morningglories

volumeeight

rivals

WORDS
NICK SPENCER

ART
JOE EISMA

COVERS
RODIN ESQUEJO

PAUL LITTLE
COLORS

JOHNNY LOWE
LETTERS

TIM DANIEL
DESIGN

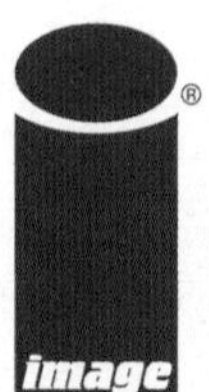

MORNING GLORIES VOL.8. FIRST PRINTING. MARCH, 2015. Published by Image Comics, Inc. Office of publication: 2001 Center St. Sixth Floor, Berkeley, CA 94704. PRINTED IN THE USA. ISBN: 978-1-63215-140-7.
For International Rights / Foreign Licensing, contact: foreignlicensing@imagecomics.com

thirty**nine**

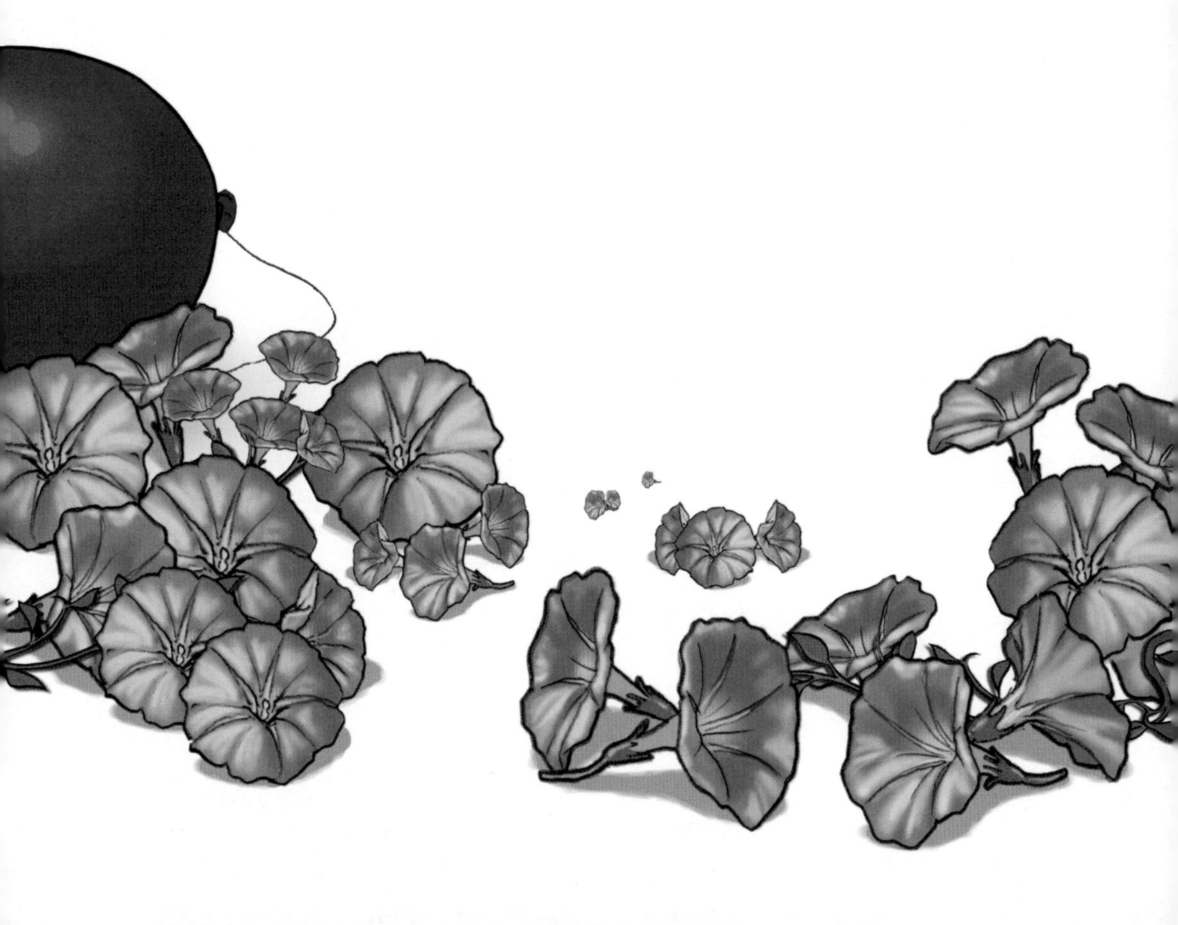

WELCOME BA

THREE MONTHS AGO.
AND SO THE GIRL WAITED FOR THE GUARDS TO RELEASE HER FOR MONTHS--
--'LET ME OUT!' SHE YELLED, OVER AND OVER AGAIN.
BUT STILL NO ONE CAME.
UNTIL ONE DAY, A STRANGER SUDDENLY APPEARED IN HER CELL, OUT OF NOWHERE.
'WHO ARE YOU?' THE GIRL ASKED. 'HAVE YOU COME TO SET ME FREE?'

'NO,' THE VISTOR REPLIED. 'ONLY YOU--'
DING DONG

DING DONG
COMING!

DING DONG DING DONG
OKAY, OKAY!

CASEY? ARE YOU--ARE YOU ALL RIGHT? WHAT'S--
I GOT IT.

I GOT *IN*, MS. CLARKSON.

I'M *GOING* AND MY PARENTS ARE *LETTING* ME, IT'S ALL REALLY *HAPPENING*--
EVERYTHING WE TALKED ABOUT, IT'S ALL COMING *TRUE* NOW.

AND IT'S ALL BECAUSE OF *YOU*, MS. CLARKSON.

NOW.
RISE AND SHINE, MORNING GLORIES!

Sloan
TODAY IS A DAY UNLIKE ANY OTHER-- BECAUSE ONLY TODAY IS TODAY!

IT'S GONNA BE WAY BETTER THAN DUMB OLD YESTERDAY! WHO NEEDS HIM, RIGHT?!!

WHY, THE ONLY THING MORE EXCITING THAN TODAY IS THE POSSIBILITY OF TOMORROW--BUT YOU CAN'T GET THERE WITHOUT--YOU GUESSED IT... TODAY!

WE'VE GOT SO MANY EXCITING NEW CHALLENGES WAITING FOR YOU, STARTING WITH...
...ATHLETES! THE INTRAMURAL TOWERBALL TOURNAMENTS ARE ABOUT TO BEGIN!

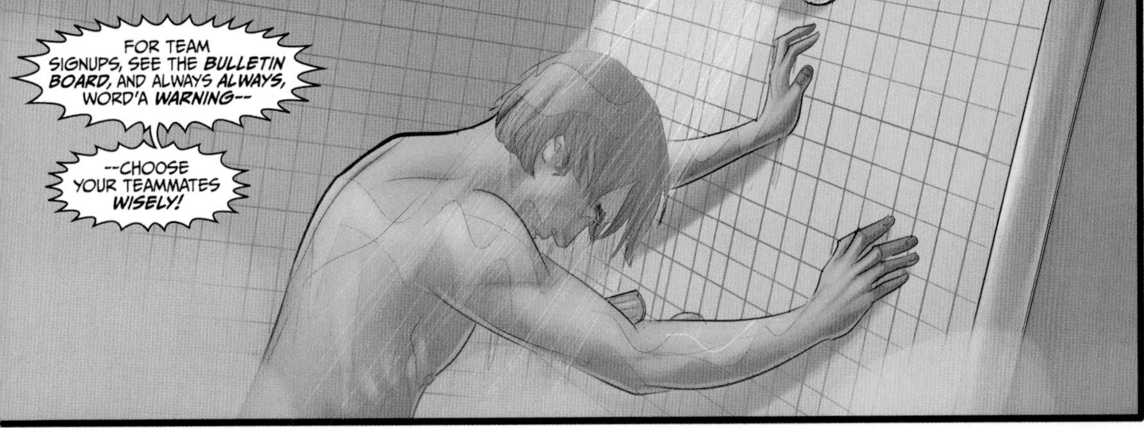
FOR TEAM SIGNUPS, SEE THE BULLETIN BOARD, AND ALWAYS ALWAYS, WORD'A WARNING--
--CHOOSE YOUR TEAMMATES WISELY!

AND SCIENCE WIZARDS! AFTER ALL THOSE DUMB NO-GOOD SHENANIGANS LAST MONTH, THE SCIENCE FAIR IS FINALLY BACK ON AND PROMISES TO BE BETTER THAN EVER THIS YEAR!
THERE'S ONLY A WEEK TO GET YOUR PROJECTS READY--

--BUT WE KNOW YOU'RE UP TO THE CHALLENGE! YOU'RE YOU, AFTER ALL!

NOW, SOME OF YOU MAY STILL BE RECOVERING FROM ALL THE RECENT EXCITEMENT, BUT THAT DOESN'T MEAN YOU WANT TO MISS OUT ON THESE UPLIFTING ACTIVITIES!

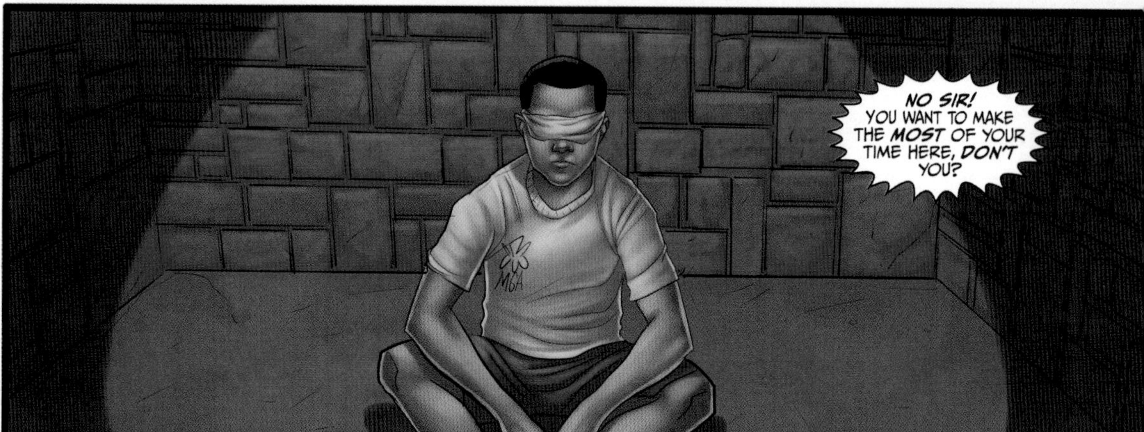
NO SIR! YOU WANT TO MAKE THE MOST OF YOUR TIME HERE, DON'T YOU?

REMEMBER, NOBODY LIKES A PARTY POOPER!

AND THE ACADEMY WANTS NOTHING MORE THAN ALL YOU HAVE TO GIVE.

THEY SEARCHED THE WORLD FAR AND WIDE, JUST TO BRING YOU HERE--

--TO THE PLACE WHERE YOU ALWAYS BELONGED!

YES SIR, HAVING YOU HERE WITH US IS THE HIGHEST HONOR ONE CAN HAVE! MAKE NO MISTAKE--

--REUNIONS ARE A SPECIAL THING!

SHE REALLY NEVER STOPS WITH THOSE ANNOUNCEMENTS, DOES SHE?

SOUNDS LIKE A PRETTY BUSY WEEK--

--YOU MIGHT EVEN HAVE TO SHOW YOUR FACE UP THERE SOON.

HELLO, CASEY.
THANKS FOR LETTING YOURSELF IN.
sigh

I'D BE WORRIED ABOUT YOU GOING THROUGH MY PAPERS, IF I HAD ANYTHING WRITTEN DOWN--
WHAT ARE YOU *TALKING* ABOUT?

'AP HISTORY PERFORMANCE REVIEW. STUDENTS OF MERIT, FAILURE RATE, ETC.'...

HM.

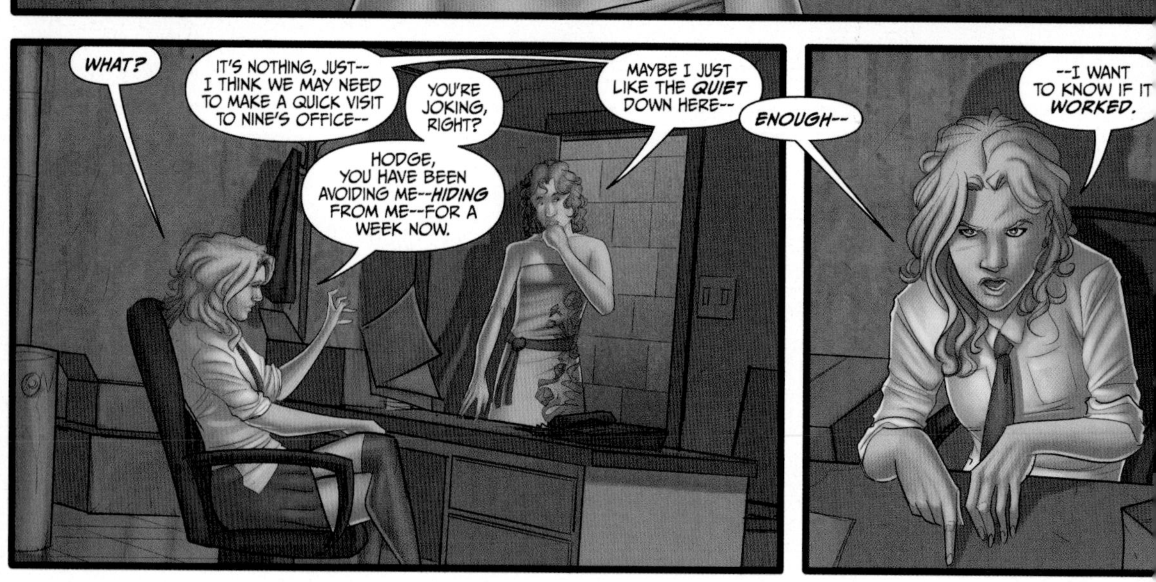
WHAT?
IT'S NOTHING, JUST-- I THINK WE MAY NEED TO MAKE A QUICK VISIT TO NINE'S OFFICE--
YOU'RE JOKING, RIGHT?
MAYBE I JUST LIKE THE *QUIET* DOWN HERE--
HODGE, YOU HAVE BEEN AVOIDING ME--*HIDING* FROM ME--FOR A WEEK NOW.
ENOUGH--
--I WANT TO KNOW IF IT *WORKED.*

CASEY--
NO, I WANT AN ANSWER!
YOU TAKE ME DOWN TO THAT CAVE, I HAVE SOME KIND OF-- HALLUCINATION, AND WAKE UP IN FRONT OF--WHATEVER THAT THING IS YOU KEEP DOWN HERE--
WITH THIS PLACE GOING TO HELL IN THE MEANTIME--
IT WAS A LOT TO TAKE IN, I UNDERSTAND.
YOU REALLY DON'T. BUT I WENT ALONG WITH ALL THIS, BECAUSE-- YOU MADE ME AN OFFER. AN OFFER THAT NEVER EXACTLY SOUNDED POSSIBLE, BUT I STILL TOOK YOU UP ON IT. PROBABLY VERY FOOLISHLY.
YOU SAID YOU COULD...YOU COULD BRING MY PARENTS BACK...
...DID YOU?
sigh
YOU REALLY DON'T REMEMBER?

THREE MONTHS AGO.
WHY DO I NEED A BLINDFOLD AGAIN?
CASEY, JESUS--I TOLD YOU. IT'S A SURPRISE.
ACCEPT NOT BEING IN CHARGE FOR THE FIRST TIME IN YOUR LIFE, CONTROL FREAK.
OKAY, BUT-- THIS HAD BETTER NOT BE SOME KIND OF SEVEN MINUTES IN HEAVEN SCENARIO.
AT LEAST PROMISE ME THAT.
GIVEN THE LAST TIME YOU TRIED THAT YOU KNEED THE GUY IN THE NUTS, PROBABLY NOT MANY TAKERS.
IT WAS A REFLEX THING.
TRUST ME, THIS WILL BE SLIGHTLY BETTER THAN THAT, CASE.
CAREFUL, WE'RE HERE--
I'LL TAKE THAT BET.

GOOD LUCK, CASEY!
SURPRISE!!

FINE.
YOU WIN.

YOU REALLY THOUGHT WE'D MISS OUT ON ONE MORE CHANCE TO DRINK IN FRONT OF YOU?
GUYS, THIS IS--
--THIS IS AMAZING. YOU REALLY GOT EVERYONE--
WELL, ALMOST--

MS. CLARKSON WANTED US TO TELL YOU HOW SORRY SHE WAS SHE COULDN'T MAKE IT.
SUCH A SHAME. REALLY.
KATH--
AW, BUT DON'T WORRY, CASE--

YOUR SECOND-FAVORITE PERSON IN THE WORLD IS HERE!

THANKS FOR COMING, ISABEL.

NOW.
WHERE ARE YOU GOING?!!
BETTER TO SHOW YOU THAN TELL YOU ON THIS ONE...

I AM SO SICK OF THESE GAMES--
WELL, I GET THE FEELING THIS TIME WON'T CHANGE YOUR MIND. BUT AT LEAST THERE'S CAKE.
CAKE?

YES-- CAKE.
Cake

NOW CAN YOU GRAB THAT BOX OVER THERE FOR ME?
WHY WOULD I...
BECAUSE I HAVE MY HANDS FULL, CASEY!

I--I CAN'T BELIEVE I'M DOING THIS...
I CAN ACTUALLY BE VERY PERSUASIVE WHEN I WANT TO BE. NOW, OVER HERE--
Cake

OH, *GOOD*-- THEY SET UP THE TABLE.
WHAT *IS* THIS PLACE?
WHAT DO YOU MEAN? IT'S THE *REC ROOM.*

GO AHEAD AND PUT THAT BOX DOWN WHEREVER.
AND *THIS* IS WHAT YOU NEEDED TO SHOW ME?
ROUNDABOUTS.
OH, THAT'S *RIGHT.* YOU ALL HAVE BEEN SO BUSY TRYING TO *DESTROY* THIS PLACE, YOU PROBABLY DIDN'T NOTICE WE GOT YOU A *POOL TABLE.*
NOW, AS A REWARD FOR YOU BEING SO HELPFUL WITH THIS STUFF, *HERE'S* WHAT HAPPENED...

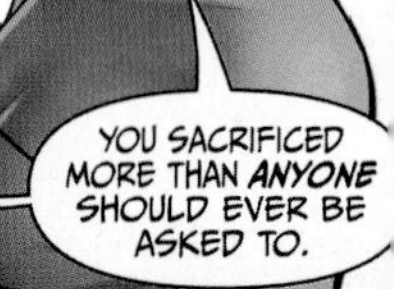
...YOU AND I WENT BACK IN YOUR PAST. THIRTEEN *YEARS* BACK, IN FACT.
MUCH FARTHER BACK THAN I'D *PLANNED,* BUT--
--IT ENDED UP *WORKING* IN OUR FAVOR.
YOU SPENT THIRTEEN YEARS PREPARING FOR THIS--FOR WHAT YOU'RE GOING TO DO *NEXT.*
YOU DID SO MANY THINGS-- SOME OF THEM *TRULY* TERRIBLE--TO MAKE SURE YOU ENDED UP RIGHT HERE IN *THIS* ROOM, RIGHT *NOW.*
YOU SACRIFICED MORE THAN *ANYONE* SHOULD EVER BE ASKED TO.

AND NOW YOU DON'T *BELIEVE* ME--
YOU'RE GODDAMNED *RIGHT* I DON'T--
AND THAT'S FINE.
YOU SEE, CASEY--

--I'M ABOUT TO *PROVE* IT.

THREE MONTHS AGO.
THANKS AGAIN FOR COMING, YOU GUYS!
I'LL SEE YOU TOMORROW--

WOW, THAT WAS ONE WILD PARTY, CASEY--
--DON'T STOP 'TIL TEN, AM I RIGHT?
ISABEL...DID MY PARENTS ACTUALLY INVITE YOU TO THIS?
OF COURSE THEY DID!
APPARENTLY, I'M ALL YOU EVER TALK ABOUT.
BUT I'M NOT SAYING ANYTHING NICE. I CAN'T BELIEVE YOU SHOWED UP HERE--

ARE YOU KIDDING?
AND MISS MY CHANCE TO SEND FOND FAREWELLS TO THE GIRL WHO CHALLENGED ME--
--INSPIRED ME--
--MADE ME WORK SO MUCH HARDER THESE LAST COUPLE OF YEARS?
IT'S LIKE YOU DON'T KNOW ME AT ALL.
IS THAT AN OPTION?
HERE WE GO...
OH, BE CIVIL. IF I CAN, GIVEN ALL YOU'VE DONE TO ME, YOU CERTAINLY CAN.

NO, NO, TONIGHT'S NOT ABOUT THE PAST, IS IT? NOT WHEN YOU HAVE SUCH A BRIGHT FUTURE AHEAD OF YOU.
MORNING GLORY ACADEMY! HOW PRESTIGIOUS.
I REALLY DIDN'T THINK YOU'D GET IN.
WELL, I WAS FIRST IN MY CLASS, WASN'T I?
NO ROOM FOR ASTERISKS ON THE APPLICATION I SUPPOSE.

OH GOD, THE SCIENCE FAIR THING AGAIN? SERIOUSLY?
WHAT YOU DID ISN'T POSSIBLE. YOU KNOW IT, DEAR, AND SO DO I.
AND YET, I DID IT.
THEN SHOW YOUR WORK.

ISABEL, ASIDE FROM THE FACT THAT I DON'T HAVE TO SHOW YOU ANYTHING--
--IT WAS A YEAR AGO. IT'S OVER.
I COULDN'T AGREE MORE. AGAIN, I AM MOVING ON WITH NOTHING BUT LOVE IN MY HEART.
SOUNDS LIKE IT.
WELL, NOW THAT WE'VE GOTTEN THROUGH THAT, I HAVE SOME ACTUAL FRIENDS TO THANK--
OF COURSE.
ONE MORE THING, THOUGH--

--I GOT YOU A CARD.
I--I DON'T EVEN...

IT'S BLANK.

IT? OH GOSH, I MUST'VE ORGOTTEN TO ACTUALLY WRITE THE MESSAGE.
I AM *SUCH* AN AIRHEAD SOMETIMES.
I SUPPOSE IT WOULD JUST BE AWKWARD TO *TELL* YOU WHAT I WAS GOING TO WRITE...
YOU KNOW WHAT, ISABEL? I WOULDN'T *BOTHER.*
I'M GOING TO *TREASURE* THIS.
I'M GOING TO KEEP IT WITH ME, *EVERYWHERE* I GO. USE IT AS A *BOOKMARK.*
SO THAT *EVERY* TIME I THINK OF YOU--

--I CAN REMEMBER *EXACTLY* HOW MUCH YOU MEAN TO ME.

WELL, AS LONG AS I'VE MADE AN *IMPRESSION.*
CONGRATULATIONS AGAIN ON GETTING ACCEPTED TO THE SCHOOL OF YOUR DREAMS. YOU *ALMOST* DESERVE IT.
WON'T BE THE *SAME* AROUND HERE WITHOUT YOU--
--IT'LL JUST BE *BETTER,* I SUPPOSE.

I *HATE* YOU.

NOW.
YOU'RE GOING TO *PROVE* I WENT BACK IN TIME?
I'M GOING TO APPEAL TO YOUR WAY OF THINKING.
SIMPLEST SOLUTION IS *USUALLY,* ET CET--
MISS HODGE?

IS THE PARTY ABOUT TO START?
FRANCINE! *YES!* COME *ON* IN.
YOU THINK W HAVE CAK *EVERY* DA AROUN HERE?
PARTY?
PARTY FOR *WHAT?*

HERE'S THE *BAD* NEWS. THE *THING* YOU'VE BEEN WORKING TOWARDS ALL THIS TIME--
--WE'RE NOT *THERE* YET.
THERE'S STILL MOR THAT NEEDS TO B DONE. AND THIS *NEX* PART IS GOING TO B THE HARDES

WE'RE MOVING INTO A DIFFERENT STAGE IN ALL THIS, AND YOU'RE GOING TO HAVE TO--
--THAT'S RIGHT, EVERYONE, *COME ON IN!*
HODGE?
YOU'RE GOING TO HAVE TO DO SOME THINGS THAT I KNOW YOU'RE NOT GOING TO *LIKE.*

NOW GIVE ME A HAND WITH THIS *BANNER.*

I CAN'T BELIEVE I'M EVEN INDULGING THIS, BUT--WHAT KIND OF THINGS?
YOU WANT OUT OF THIS PLACE. YOU WANT IT DESTROYED.
YOU WANT TO UNDO THE DAMAGE IT'S CAUSED IN YOUR LIFE.
AND YOU THINK YOU'LL DO ANYTHING TO MAKE THAT HAPPEN.

BUT WHAT IF I TOLD YOU, IN ORDER TO ACCOMPLISH ALL THAT, YOU WOULD NEED TO BECOME A PART OF THIS PLACE? THAT INSTEAD OF SETTING YOURSELF APART FROM IT, YOU NEED TO INGRATIATE YOURSELF WITHIN IT--
I WOULD NEVER--
THEN THIS WHOLE THING IS DOOMED TO FAILURE. YOU REALLY WANT TO BE THAT STUBBORN? WAIT, I FORGOT WHO I'M ASKING--

--I KNOW YOU THINK I'M PLAYING SOME GAME HERE, BUT THERE HAS TO BE ANOTHER PART OF YOU THAT DIDN'T LOSE EVERYTHING YOU WENT THROUGH--
--THAT KNOWS I'M TELLING YOU THE TRUTH.
WELCOME BACK!!
HODGE, WHAT IS THIS PARTY FOR?
WE'RE WELCOMING BACK YOUR CLASS PRESIDENT.

MY WHAT?
YOUR STUDENT COUNCIL CLASS PRESIDENT.
AND WHO IS THAT?
SSSH! SHE'S COMING DOWN THE HALL NOW!

HODGE...
REMEMBER WHAT I JUST SAID ABOUT STUFF YOU'RE NOT GONNA LIKE?
OH MY GOD, IS ALL THIS FOR ME?!!

WELCOME BACK, ISABEL!!!

YOU GOTTA BE FUCKING KIDDING ME.
OME
K!!

WOW, I JUST--
--I DON'T EVEN KNOW WHAT TO SAY.
ALL OF YOU--YOU'RE JUST SO AMAZING. I CAN'T TELL HOW GOOD IT FEELS TO BE SURROUNDED BY FRIENDS.

OH, AND SPEAKING OF--
IS THAT--CASEY?
CASEY BLEVINS?
I CAN'T BELIEVE MY OWN--

--WELL--
SLAM!
--IT IS AN EMOTIONAL MOMENT FOR ALL OF US, I SUPPOSE.

CASEY--WAIT--
FOR WHAT?
ANOTHER ONE OF YOUR STUPID GAMES?
WHAT DO YOU THINK JUST HAPPENED IN THERE?

WHAT DO YOU MEAN?
YOU RECRUITED THE BITCHY GIRL FROM MY OLD SCHOOL. GREAT.
AND HERE I THOUGHT THIS PLACE COULDN'T GET ANY WORSE. SHE'LL FIT RIGHT IN, BEING AROUND HER IS ONLY SLIGHTLY BETTER THAN BEING TASERED.
NO, THAT'S NOT-- I ALREADY TOLD YOU.
ISABEL ISN'T NEW HERE...SHE'S YOUR CLASS PRESIDENT.
NO, SHE-- SHE WENT TO MY OLD SCHOOL!
FOR TWO YEARS, SHE DID. BEFORE THAT, THOUGH, THE ENTIRETY OF HER ACADEMIC CAREER WAS SPENT HERE.
HOW'S THAT WORK?
SHE WAS RE-ELECTED IN ABSENTIA TWICE.
GIRL'S POPULAR.
NO, I MEAN--HOW WOULD YOU KNOW TO PLANT HER AT MY SCHOOL SO LONG BEFORE I EVEN THOUGHT ABOUT, MUCH LESS APPLIED TO-- OH GOD--
--MS. CLARKSON?
NO...SHE--SHE WAS ONE OF YOURS, WASN'T SHE?
I THOUGHT SHE WAS-- I THOUGHT SHE WAS MY FRIEND!
OH, SHE WAS. KINDA. IT'S A LOT MORE COMPLICATED THAN THAT.
MAYBE IF WE GO TO THE NURSE'S OFFICE, SOME OF THIS WILL START COMING BACK TO YOU--
I CAN'T BELIEVE YOU--YOU SENT HER TO SELL ME ON THE SCHOOL IN THE FIRST PLACE-- ALL THAT, BUT--
--WHY?
WHAT THE HELL DO YOU PEOPLE WANT WITH US?!!
ME, PERSONALLY?--

--I WANT YOU TO RUN AGAINST ISABEL FOR CLASS PRESIDENT.

...AND WE'RE DONE HERE.
CASEY, PLEASE, JUST LISTEN TO ME--
--REMEMBER WHAT I SAID BEFORE, ABOUT YOU NEEDING TO BECOME A PART OF THIS PLACE?
I AM NOT RUNNING FOR YOUR STUPID STUDENT COUNCIL OR WHATEVER IT IS! THIS IS RIDICULOUS--

IT ISN'T. WE TAKE STUDENT GOVERNMENT SERIOUSLY HERE.
WE'RE YOUR SERVANTS, AFTER ALL, REMEMBER?
THESE LEADERSHIP POSITIONS, THEY COME WITH SOME VERY REAL RESPONSIBILITIES--
THIS ONE YOU'LL PROBABLY BE MORE INTERESTED IN--
I'M SURE THE RITUAL SACRIFICE COMMITTEE WILL DO FINE WITHOUT ME.

FROM THE MINUTE YOU ARRIVED HERE, YOU'VE BEEN TOLD THIS IS ALL BY SOMEONE'S DESIGN. THAT THERE'S SOMEONE WE ALL ANSWER TO, AND FOLLOW WITHOUT QUESTION.
THE HEADMASTER...
RIGHT...
YOU KNOW, I'M STARTING TO DOUBT THIS GUY IS EVEN REAL--
MY FATHER CERTAINLY EXISTS, I CAN ASSURE YOU.
BUT HERE'S THE THING, CASEY--NO STUDENT HERE CAN ADDRESS HIM, OR EVEN BE IN HIS PRESENCE--
NO STUDENT--

--EXCEPT THE CLASS PRESIDENT.

"TAKE THE DAY TO THINK ABOUT THIS, CASEY--"

"--NOW THAT YOU KNOW THE STAKES."

"BEATING ISABEL WOULDN'T BE EASY, BUT YOU'RE A RESOURCEFUL **GIRL.**"

"WHO KNOWS?"
for Casey

"MAYBE YOU WON'T EVEN **HAVE** TO CHEAT THIS TIME."

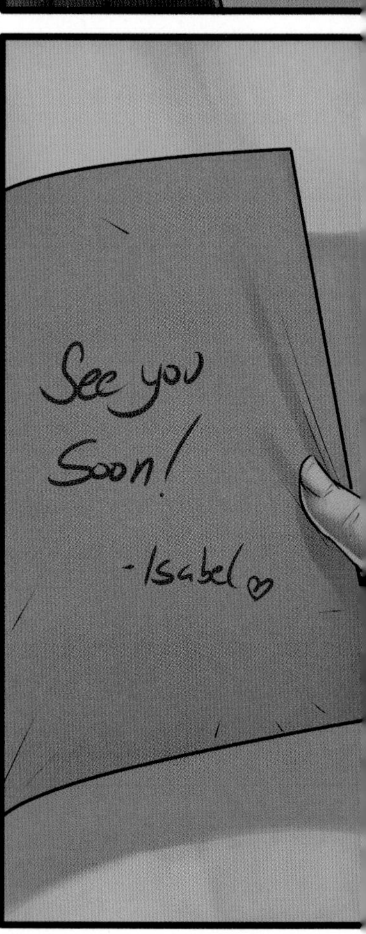
See you
Soon!
-Isabel

forty

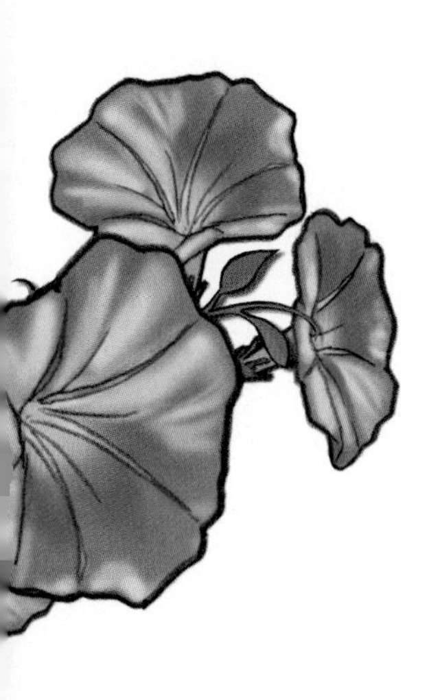

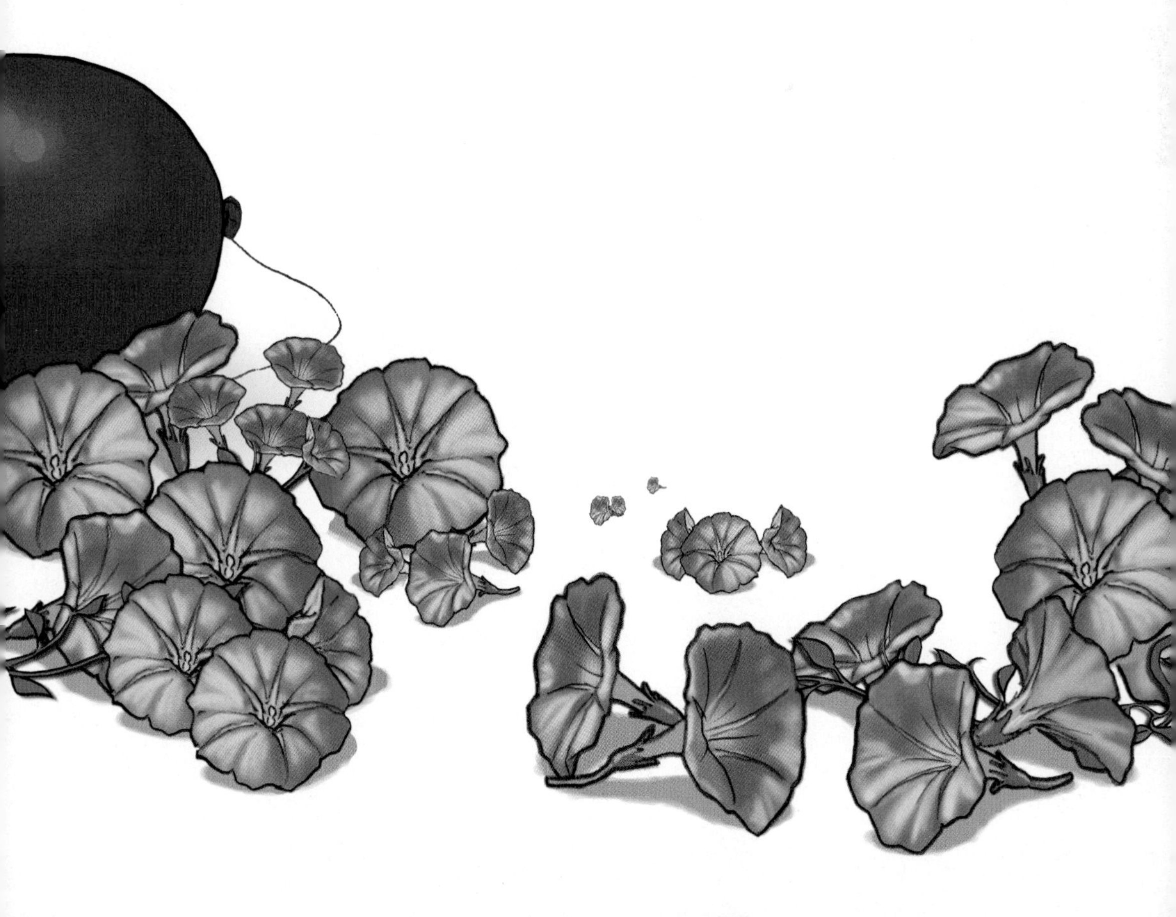

I'M JUST SAYING WE SHOULD TALK ABOUT IT--
MORE. TALK ABOUT IT MORE, YOU MEAN.
SINCE IT DIDN'T GO YOUR WAY THE LAST TIME.
BECAUSE THEY LISTEN TO YOU--
AND WHY DO YOU SUPPOSE THAT IS, CONFUSED GUY?
I THOUGHT THE WHOLE POINT OF THIS NEWSPAPER THING--
THE ANSWER.

--ANOTHER THING YOU JUST DECIDED, THE NAME--I MEAN--
--I THOUGHT WE WERE DOING THIS TO TELL THE TRUTH ABOUT THIS PLACE, OR WHATEVER--YOU KNOW, TO HELP PEOPLE--
AND WE ARE.
THE RIGHT WAY.

YOU MEAN YOUR WAY.
I FAIL TO SEE THE DIFFERENCE. BUT IF YOU HAVE SUCH A PROBLEM, PERHAPS OUR LITTLE GANG ISN'T THE BEST PLACE FOR--
ALL RIGHT, STUDENTS, QUIET NOW--

AS YOU KNOW, NEXT WEEK WE'LL BE HOSTING OUR ANNUAL SCIENCE FAIR.
AND SINCE IT'S BEEN RESCHEDULED AFTER THAT BIT OF UNPLEASANTNESS LAST MONTH TO A DATE LATER IN THE TERM THAN WE KNOW YOU'D LIKE, WE'VE DECIDED THAT, RATHER THAN PUNISHING EVERYONE FOR THE ACTIONS OF A FEW--
--WE'D INSTEAD LIKE TO OFFER YOU SOME ADDITIONAL ASSISTANCE WITH YOUR PROJECTS.
TO THAT END, WE'VE INVITED A PAIR OF HIGHLY QUALIFIED GUEST TEACHERS TO JOIN US TEMPORARILY, TO HELP INSPIRE YOU AND GUIDE YOU THROUGH THE PROCESS!

NOW, THESE GUESTS ARE THE PRE-EMINENT MINDS IN THEIR RESPECTIVE FIELDS, AND MORE THAN UP TO THE TASK AT HAND, BUT AT THE SAME TIME, THEY ARE NEW HERE AND AS SUCH, MAY PROVE A BIT UNFAMILIAR WITH OUR WAYS--
--I HOPE YOU'LL ALL DO EVERYTHING YOU CAN TO MAKE THEM FEEL COMFORTABLE AND AT HOME HERE WITH US. IT TRULY IS OUR HONOR TO HAVE THEM!
SO, PLEASE, JOIN ME IN GIVING AN ENTHUSIASTIC WELCOME--

--TO DOCTORS IAN SIMON AND ELLEN RICHMOND!

BUT DUDE--THAT'S YOUR--
NOW, LET'S NOT MAKE A BIG ISSUE OF THIS--
MOM!!!

VANESSA--
...YOU WILL BE A BIT...
...A COUPLE OF YOU MAY BE A BIT MORE *FAMILIAR* WITH OUR VISITORS.
WHAT ARE YOU *DOING* HERE? ARE YOU--ARE YOU *OKAY?*
I'M *FINE,* SWEETHEART. ARE *YOU?*
I'M JUST-- I DON'T KNOW IF I *SHOULD* BE, BUT--I'M *SO* GLAD YOU'RE HERE.
A-*HRM.*
IAN.
SIR.
I--
--YOU LOOK WELL.
TALLER.
GOOD, THEN.
I--I TRUST YOU HAVEN'T UP TO ANY *TROUBLE?*
OF COURSE NOT. YOU KNOW ME--
--DAD.

THE DAY BEFORE.
"OKAY, SO, JUST TO GET THIS OUT OF THE WAY--THE FIRST EDITION OF *THE ANSWER* IS *OUT* THERE. AND OUR LITTLE 'NEWSPAPER' IS A *HUGE SUCCESS.*

"EVERYBODY THAT'S ANYBODY IS READING IT.
"OUR FIRST HEADLINE--THE ARRIVAL OF THE *SCIENTISTS*--HAS GOT THEM TALKING.

"SOMETHING THAT'S NEVER HAPPENED IN THE HISTORY OF THIS PLACE IS *FINALLY* HERE--
"--THE STUDENTS ARE GETTING THEIR *OWN* MESSAGE OUT.

"BUT BEFORE WE STARTED PATTING EACH OTHER ON THE BACK, I'D *WARN* YOU--
"--ANY CELEBRATION IS *WAY* PREMATURE. AFTER *ALL*--"

--WE DON'T EVEN HAVE ANYTHING FOR OUR SECOND EDITION.
SO, PLEASE-- ANYBODY? WE NEED IDEAS.

THE STUDENT COUNCIL ELECTIONS ARE COMING UP...
PSH! WHAT ELECTION? ISABEL WILL RUN UNOPPOSED, AS ALWAYS. THE DICTATORSHIP PERSEVERES.
WAIT--WHO'S ISABEL?

DON'T LOOK AT ME. SHE'S BEEN 'STUDYING ABROAD' OR SOMETHING SINCE BEFORE I GOT HERE.
THE LESS YOU KNOW OF HER, HUNTER, THE BETTER.
SHE'S WHAT HAPPENS WHEN YOU'VE BEEN AT THIS PLACE SINCE THE AGE OF FIVE.
I'D SAY IT ISN'T PRETTY... BUT SHE IS ACTUALLY QUITE STUNNING.

POINT IS, THE ELECTION IS A SHAM. SHE DIDN'T EVEN NEED TO BE HERE TO WIN--
--THE WHOLE THING WILL JUST BE A BIG ASS-KISSING PARADE NOW THAT SHE'S BACK.
SO IF THAT'S ALL WE'VE GOT--
ACTUALLY, I MIGHT HAVE SOMETHING--

SERIOUSLY?
WHAT?
NO, IT'S JUST--THERE IS LITERALLY NO ONE HERE THAT KNOWS LESS ABOUT WHAT IS GOING ON IN THIS PLACE THAN YOU DO.
THE GUY THAT MAKES THE AMAZON DELIVERIES KNOWS MORE THAN YOU.

sigh
IT'S JUST--I HEARD A COUPLE OF THE GUARDS TALKING--
--APPARENTLY MS. DARAMOUNT WENT NUTS ON ONE OF THE KIDS THEY'RE KEEPING IN THE CELLS.
UH, HUNTER... THAT IS NOT EXACTLY UNCOMMON IN THIS PLACE--
NO, I GET THAT--BUT--HERE'S THE THING--
--I DON'T KNOW WHO HE IS, BUT YOU--YOU GUYS DO--ESPECIALLY YOU, IAN--
JAMAICA

"--HIS NAME IS FORTUNATO."

ER, WELL, YES, GREETINGS, EVERYONE.
AS WAS JUST POINTED OUT, I AM DOCTOR OLIVER SIMON.
WHAT I'D LIKE US TO DO--IN OUR HOPEFULLY LIMITED TIME TOGETHER--
--IS NOT JUST SOMETHING TO APPEASE YOUR CAPTORS--

--AH, FORGIVE ME--
--YOUR TEACHERS. TEACHERS...
...EASY TO CONFUSE THE TWO, ESPECIALLY AT THE AGE YOU'RE AT...
...AS I WAS SAYING, I'D LIKE US TO ATTEMPT SOMETHING WORTHY OF YOU. TO REALLY THINK AND DREAM BIG, AS IT WERE.
SO I SUPPOSE THE QUESTION TO BEGIN WITH SHOULD BE--

WHAT IS REALITY?
--WHAT...
...IS...
...REALITY?

ANYONE?
THOUGHTS?
YES, YOU--
PHILIP K. DICK SAID REALITY IS THE STUFF THAT, WHEN YOU STOP BELIEVING IN IT, DOESN'T GO AWAY.
AND IT'S A VERY CLEVER ANSWER.
REALITY IS A VERY STUBBORN BEAST. GOOD PLACE TO START.

--BUT NOT QUITE COMPLETE ENOUGH TO SATISFY US.
AFTER ALL, THERE ARE MANY THINGS WE'D REGARD AS REAL--THINGS LIKE THE STOCK MARKET, FOR INSTANCE--
--THAT IF WE ALL STOPPED BELIEVING IN THEM, WOULD IN FACT, CEASE TO BE.
NO, WE NEED A DEFINITION THAT'S MORE ALL-ENCOMPASSING, SOMETHING THAT DOESN'T GET TRAPPED BY ABSTRACTS OR CONSTRUCTS.
ANYONE?

THE FUNDAMENTAL BUILDING BLOCKS. THE SMALLEST UNIT YOU CAN BREAK SOMETHING DOWN TO.
AH, YES--NOW, THIS ***CAN*** WORK, BUT IT'S AWFULLY ***PROHIBITIVE.*** IT MEANS WE NO LONGER VIEW THIS CLASSROOM, ***OR*** THIS BUILDING, OR THE GROUND IT'S BUILT ON AS ***REAL***--
--INSTEAD, ALL THAT ***COUNTS*** IS WHAT'S UNDER, WHAT'S BELOW.
AND, MORE ***FRUSTRATINGLY***--

--IT'S ACTUALLY THESE ***SMALLEST*** INGREDIENTS THAT POSE THE MOST DIFFICULTY FOR US IN DETERMINING WHAT REALITY ***IS.***
THAT'S ALL THANKS TO WHAT'S REFERRED TO IN QUANTUM PHYSICS AS 'WAVE-PARTICLE DUALITY.'
DOES ANYONE KNOW WHAT THAT IS?

THE SMALLEST PARTICLES EXHIBIT PROPERTIES OF MORE THAN ONE STATE. THEY EXIST IN A SUPERPOSITION.
THAT'S RIGHT.
TO PUT IT ANOTHER WAY--AN ELECTRON CAN MOVE IN ***TWO*** DIRECTIONS AT ONCE. BE IN TWO ***PLACES*** AT ONCE.
NOW, THAT DOESN'T SOUND LIKE REALITY AT ***ALL,*** DOES IT? HOW CAN ***ANYTHING*** EXIST IN AN UNDETERMINED STATE?
AND KEEP IN ***MIND,*** THIS APPLIES TO EVERYTHING YOU SEE ***AROUND*** YOU. WE AND ALL THAT'S AROUND US, WE'RE ***MADE*** OF ELECTRONS AND THE LIKE. IT'S ALL BUILT ON THIS SHAKY ***FOUNDATION.***

AND HERE'S THE TRULY MAD BIT--WHEN ANY ATTEMPT IS MADE TO OBSERVE AN ELECTRON IN THIS MURKY, CONFUSED STATE--IT COLLAPSES!
CHOOSES ONE LOCATION, ONE DIRECTION.
BECOMES SOMETHING REAL AND FIXED.
THIS IS WHAT IS KNOWN AS THE COPENHAGEN INTERPRETATION OF QUANTUM PHYSICS, AS LAID OUT BY THE GREAT PHYSICIST, NIELS BOHR.

THE ASSERTION IS A FANTASTIC ONE--THAT FOR SOMETHING TO BE REAL, AS WE'D CONVENTIONALLY DEFINE IT AT LEAST, IT MUST BE OBSERVED.
AND HOW ELSE CAN WE DEFINE OBSERVATION BUT AS THE ACT OF A CONSCIOUS MIND?

SO DEFINING REALITY BY OUR SMALLEST INGREDIENTS ENDS UP TURNING THE QUESTION RIGHT BACK UPON US--
--WE DETERMINE THEIR STATE, RATHER THAN THEM DETERMINING OURS.
AT LEAST, THAT WAS THE BELIEF OF MAX PLANCK, THE ORIGINATOR OF QUANTUM THEORY--

--IT WAS PLANCK WHO SAID, 'I REGARD MATTER AS DERIVATIVE FROM CONSCIOUSNESS.'

GUYS, COME ON. THIS IS OBVIOUS.
IT'S A TRAP.

CUE ACKBAR IMPRESSION.
I DON'T GET IT. WHAT KIND OF TRAP?
I DO NOT SEE IT AS WELL, IAN.

OH COME ON-- NOW THAT THE ANSWER IS OUT THERE, WE'VE GOT THEM RUNNING SCARED. THERE'S A MEANS OF COMMUNICATION THEY DON'T CONTROL.
SO WHAT WILL THEY DO? TRY TO FIND SOME WAY TO MANIPULATE IT. MAKE IT SERVE THEIR OWN ENDS.
OR--

--TRY TO FLUSH OUT WHO'S PUTTING THE PAPER TOGETHER IN THE FIRST PLACE.
WAIT, YOU THINK THEY LET ME OVERHEAR THEM, ON PURPOSE?
OF COURSE I DO! I MEAN, COME ON--
THE DAY AFTER OUR FIRST HEADLINE, AND THEN THE GUARDS-- WHO NEVER GO OFF THE 'YOU ARE NUMBER SIX' SCRIPT-- ARE SUDDENLY CHATTING ABOUT BASEMENT DETAILS?
YOU ASK ME--

"--SOUNDS A BIT TOO CONVENIENT."
SO WE HAVE OUR PROBLEM--WHAT WE CONSIDER TO BE THE MATERIAL WORLD IS NOTHING OF THE SORT WHEN LEFT TO ITS OWN DEVICES, AND INSTEAD WHAT WE WOULD CONSIDER THE EPHEMERAL--CONSCIOUSNESS--
--APPEARS TO BEAR RESPONSIBILITY FOR ALL WE'D CALL REALITY.
WHAT THEN, DOES A UNIVERSE OPERATING UNDER THOSE RULES LOOK LIKE?
HOW CAN WE SAVE OURSELVES FROM THIS DILEMMA?

YES, IN THE BACK--
WHAT IS REALITY?
THIS IS THE 'MANY WORLDS' IDEA, RIGHT?
AND THAT IS?

THE IDEA THAT, INSTEAD OF EVERYTHING BEING UNDETERMINED UNTIL IT'S OBSERVED, IT'S ACTUALLY JUST BOTH--AND THE UNIVERSE SPLITS IN TWO WITH EACH OBSERVATION.
MM--SO OUR CHOICES WERE A AND B, AND WE OBSERVED A, BUT THERE'S ANOTHER UNIVERSE WHERE IT'S B.
AND SO ON AND SO FORTH, FOR EVERY CHOICE IMAGINABLE AND EVERY UNIT OF QUANTA, MULTIPLYING AND BRANCHING OUT INFINITELY!

WELL, THIS CERTAINLY PUTS US IN A DIFFERENT PLACE ALTOGETHER, DOESN'T IT? PERHAPS WE'VE SOLVED IT. TO BE SURE, THE MANY-WORLDS INTERPRETATION ISN'T ALL GOOD NEWS--WORLDS WHERE HITLER WON THE WAR OR WHAT HAVE YOU, BUT AT LEAST WE'VE CLEARED UP THE LUDICROUS PROBLEM OF CONSCIOUSNESS DETERMINING THE UNIVERSE, HAVEN'T WE?

NOW THE OBSERVATION IS MERELY A FORK IN THE ROAD ON A PHYSICAL MAP THAT'S BEYOND OUR CONTROL.
THAT SOUNDS A BIT MORE LIKE REALITY, DOESN'T IT?
BUT WE MIGHT NOT BE OUT OF THE WOODS JUST YET...
...CONSIDER A UNIVERSE ABSENT US. ABSENT ANY FORM OF CONSCIOUS LIFE, IN FACT.
NO OBSERVERS, AS IT WERE.
DO ANY OF YOU SEE THE PROBLEM YET?
YES?
THE MANY WORLDS INTERPRETATION DOESN'T WORK ANYMORE.
AND WHY NOT?
BECAUSE-- NO ONE'S OBSERVING.
NOTHING'S SPLITTING OFF.
PRECISELY! BUT EVEN MORE THAN THAT--WHAT HAPPENED TO OUR FRIEND, THE ELECTRON FROM EARLIER?
WITHOUT ANYONE TO OBSERVE HIM?
HE'S TRAPPED IN THAT UNREAL STATE.
AH, SO, ONCE AGAIN--ONE UNIVERSE OR MANY, IT DOESN'T APPEAR TO MATTER, DOES IT?

NONE OF IT IS REAL WITHOUT US.

AH, *INSECURE GUY!* I'M **SO** GLAD YOU KNOW WHERE MY ROOM IS.
I'M ABOUT TO TAKE A NAP.
AND I SHOULD ***TUCK*** YOU IN?
MAYBE YOU SHOULD...UM...TAKE A NAP, TOO.

SORRY?
IT'S ABOUT-- THE DUDE DOWNSTAIRS...

AH, ***GOT*** YOU.
FINE, FINE, GIVE ME A FEW MINUTES, AND ***NAP*** BUDDIES IT IS.

sigh
ALL RIGHT THEN--

--MIGHT AS WELL GET THIS ***OVER*** WITH.

SO, I KNOW YOU SAID TO LET IT GO--
I DID.
--BUT, THEN, EARLIER TODAY, I HEARD THOSE GUARDS TALKING AGAIN, AND THEY EVEN MENTIONED WHAT CELL HE'S IN--
IMAGINE THAT.
ALMOST LIKE THEY WANTED YOU TO HEAR.

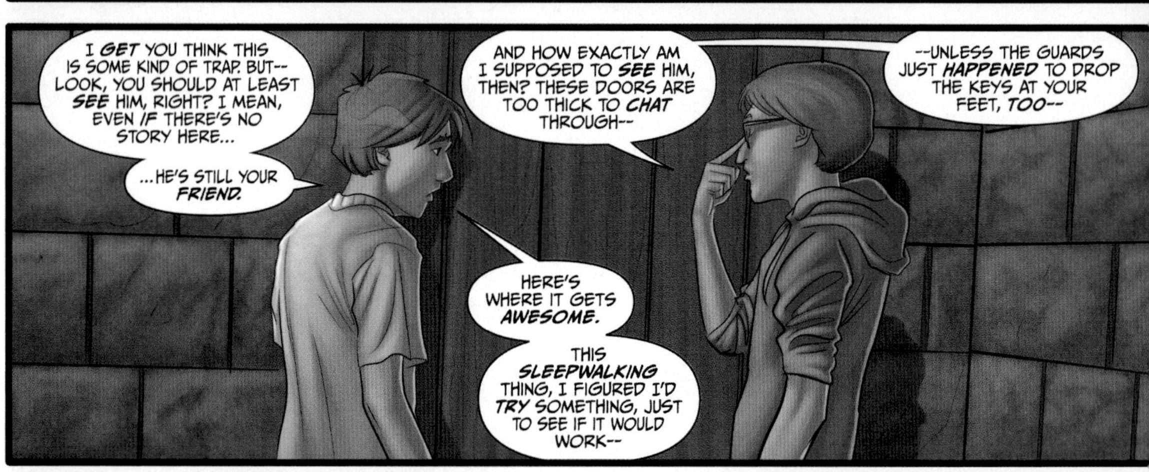

I GET YOU THINK THIS IS SOME KIND OF TRAP. BUT-- LOOK, YOU SHOULD AT LEAST SEE HIM, RIGHT? I MEAN, EVEN IF THERE'S NO STORY HERE...
...HE'S STILL YOUR FRIEND.
AND HOW EXACTLY AM I SUPPOSED TO SEE HIM, THEN? THESE DOORS ARE TOO THICK TO CHAT THROUGH--
--UNLESS THE GUARDS JUST HAPPENED TO DROP THE KEYS AT YOUR FEET, TOO--
HERE'S WHERE IT GETS AWESOME.
THIS SLEEPWALKING THING, I FIGURED I'D TRY SOMETHING, JUST TO SEE IF IT WOULD WORK--

--AND IT TOTALLY DID.
OPEN SESAME.
C-CHNK

NICE, RIGHT?
VERY. BUT--HOLD ON--

LOOK, I KNOW FORTUNATO. HE'S NOT THE MOST TALKATIVE GUY ON HIS BEST DAY.
IF WHAT YOU SAID IS TRUE, AND HE'S BEEN GETTING TORTURED DOWN HERE, I DON'T THINK HE'S GONNA OPEN UP IF SOME KID HE'S NEVER MET IS IN THERE TRYING TO GRILL HIM FOR A STORY.
HE MIGHT OPEN UP TO A FRIEND, THOUGH.
SO IF YOU REALLY WANT THIS, BEST TO LET ME HANDLE IT ALONE. AT LEAST AT FIRST--

--TRUST ME ON THIS ONE.

THANK YOU.
NOW, WHAT DO WE HAVE--

--HELL.

SO AS WE CONSIDER OUR PROJECTS FOR THIS-- FAIR THEY'RE PUTTING ON... I'D LIKE TO CHALLENGE ALL OF YOU TO ATTEMPT SOMETHING AROUND THIS THEME--
--THE CURIOUS PLACE THAT WE, THE CONSCIOUS OBSERVERS, PLAY IN THE UNIVERSE--

--AND HOW WE IMPACT THE VERY FABRIC OF REALITY WITH EVERY DECISION, EVERY--
IT'S BOLLOCKS.

UM-- IAN?
SORRY, JUST-- WHAT YOU WERE SAYING BEFORE, IT DOESN'T ADD UP.
AH--HOW SO, EXACTLY?

WELL, YOU ASKED ABOUT WHAT THE UNIVERSE WOULD LOOK LIKE WITHOUT US--
--AND BASICALLY SAID IT WASN'T REALITY BECAUSE EVERYTHING IS AN INDETERMINATE STATE.
BUT THAT'S NOT TRUE.

THE OBSERVATION CAUSES A COLLAPSE, OR A SPLIT, WHATEVER YOU THINK IT IS, BUT NO MATTER WHAT, IT'S STILL AN ELECTRON.
IT HAS THE MASS AND CHARGE, YEAH?

OF COURSE. BUT-- IT HAS NO POSITION. NO LOCATION. NO DIRECTION.
IT'S RELATIONSHIP TO THE UNIVERSE IS UNDETERMINED.
NO, IT ISN'T--
IS REALITY

WITHOUT THE OBSERVERS, IT'S EVERYTHING. ALL THOSE POTENTIAL UNIVERSES, THEY JUST ALL EXIST. AT ONCE. AND EVERYWHERE, SIMULTANEOUSLY.
TO QUOTE OUR BENEVOLENT OVERLORDS--
--ALL TOGETHER, ONE AND ALL.

ER, YES--AND TELL ME, IAN, DOES THAT SOUND LIKE THE REALITY TO YOU? AN UNDEFINED, UNDIFFERENTIATED SINGULARITY?
WHO KNOWS?

MIGHT BE BETTER THAN THIS ONE.

sigh
JUST LOOK AT YOU, FORTUNATO--

MM. NICE CELL YOU'VE GOT HERE, BROTHER.
BUT THEN I GUESS YOU CAN'T.
...IAN?

IAN, HAVE YOU-- ARE YOU HERE TO RESCUE ME?
RESCUE YOU? HMM, NOW, LET'S CONSIDER THAT ONE, SHALL WE? REMIND ME, HOW DID IT GO THAT TIME YOU RESCUED AKIKO?

PLEASE-- BROTHER--YOU HAVE TO HELP ME...
SHE'S BRAIN DEAD, DID YOU KNOW THAT? NEEDS MACHINES TO KEEP BREATHING.
AKIKO?
IAN, NO, THAT ISN'T TRUE--
SHE HAS BEEN HERE. SHE VISITS ME HERE.
YOU ARE MISTAKEN.

IT'S A TERRIBLE THING TO LOVE SOMEONE WHO DOESN'T LOVE YOU BACK.
I SUPPOSE YOU WOULDN'T KNOW MUCH ABOUT THAT--JESUS MAY NOT GIVE TWO SHITS ABOUT YOU, BUT AT LEAST HE'S NOT HERE TO TELL YOU AS MUCH.
FOR ME, THOUGH--THESE LAST FEW YEARS HAVEN'T BEEN A LOT OF FUN, BELIEVE IT OR NOT.
WATCHING HER FAWN OVER YOU WHILE I JUST HAD TO STAND THERE, LIKE AN IDIOT. MAKING JOKES.
THE FRIEND.
HUMILIATING.

BUT I GUESS THINGS HAVE A WAY OF TURNING AROUND, DON'T THEY?
KARMIC.
YOU DO SEEM TO BE PAYING A HEAVY PRICE FOR THE THINGS YOU'VE DONE--TO HER, TO ME--
I'M AFRAID I'VE DECIDED IT'S NOT ENOUGH, THOUGH.
GNN

DARAMOUNT WANTS TO MAKE AN EXAMPLE OF YOU. USE YOU TO SHOW EVERYONE HOW BIG AND TERRIBLE SHE STILL IS. IT'S PATHETIC, REALLY--BUT I'VE DECIDED TO GIVE HER HER HEADLINE.
LET YOU HAVE YOUR MOMENT IN THE SUN.
IT'LL BE THE LAST ONE YOU EVER GET, THOUGH, I'M AFRAID.
QUITE ENOUGH ATTENTION FOR YOU.
IAN--
GGG
--NO-- PLEASE--

OH, ARE YOU WORRIED I'M GOING TO HURT YOU, FORTUNATO? KILL YOU?
WELL, THAT WOULD BE THE EASY PART. YOU SEE, I WANT SO MUCH MORE THAN THAT. I'VE DECIDED TO TAKE DEAR OLD DAD'S ADVICE-- DARE TO THINK BIG. DREAM BIG.
NO, WHEN THE TIME COMES, I'M NOT JUST GOING TO TAKE YOUR LIFE, BROTHER. I'M GOING TO SET THINGS RIGHT. MAKE THINGS THE WAY THEY'RE SUPPOSED TO BE--

--I'M GOING TO MAKE IT SO YOU NEVER EXISTED IN THE FIRST PLACE.

RRRRRIINNNGG!!!
WHAT IS REALITY
AH, NEXT TIME--NEXT TIME, MS. RICHMOND WILL WALK YOU THROUGH--

--HELL, DO THEY ALWAYS IGNORE US LIKE THIS?
WHAT IS REALITY?

EALIT
I'LL DO IT.
SORRY?
THE STORY. WE'LL RUN IT--BUT I'LL WRITE IT. UNDERSTOOD?
YEAH, NO, SOUNDS FAIR, BUT--WHAT CHANGED YOUR MIND EXACTLY?
LIKE THE MAN SAID--

WHAT

"--DREAM BIG."
RESTRICTED

HELLO, YOU UGLY BEAST--

I HAVE SOME THINGS I'D LIKE YOU TO DO FOR ME.

fortyone

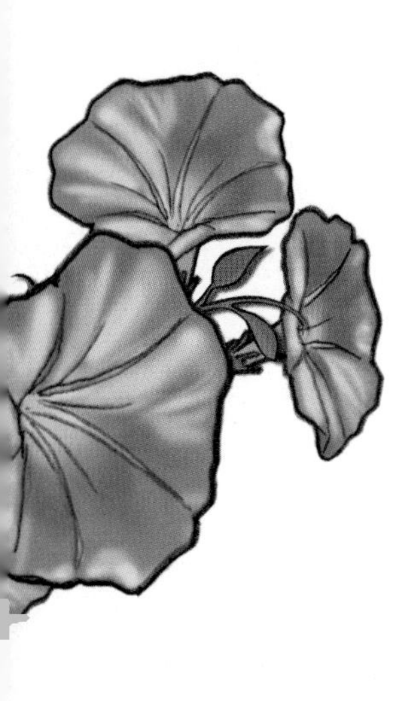

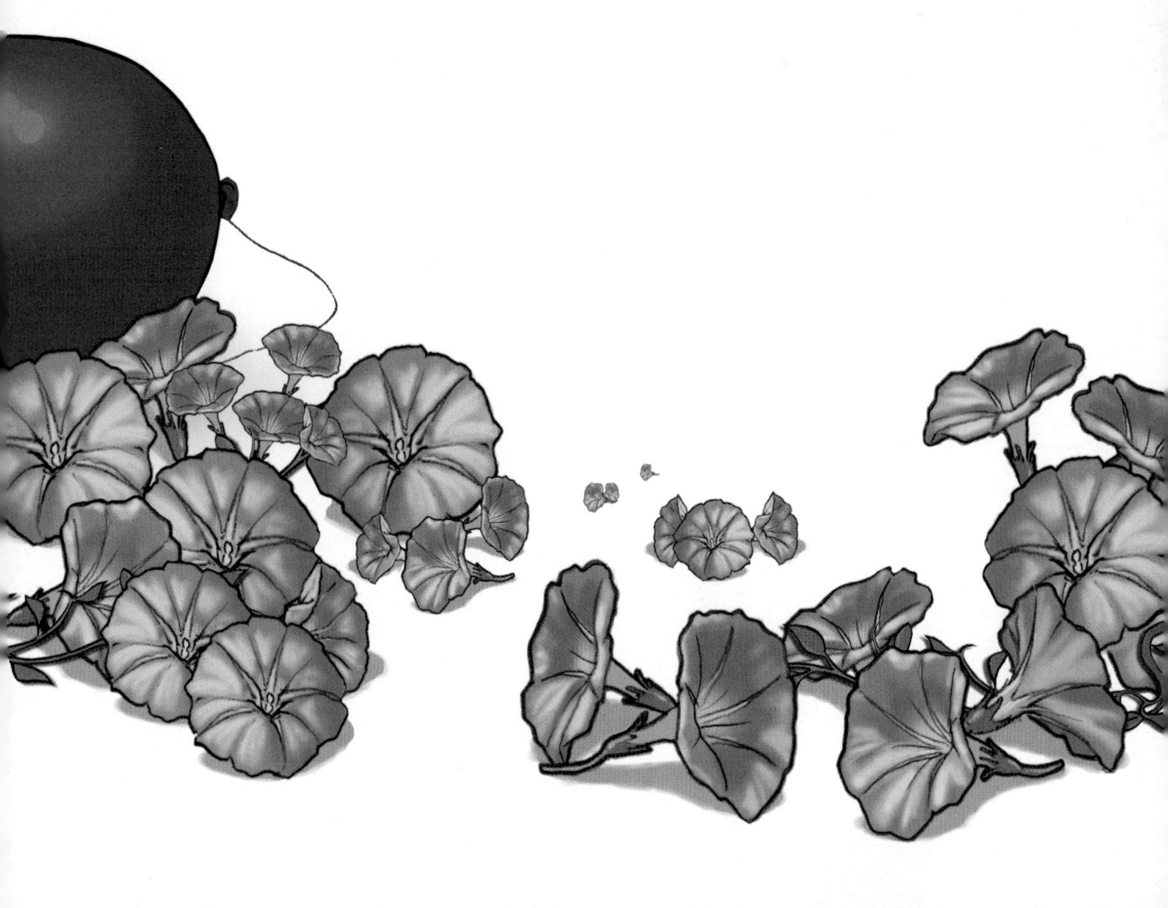

TWO YEARS AGO.

GUILLAUME?

I--I'M SORRY, I SAW YOUR LIGHT WAS STILL ON, I WANTED TO MAKE SURE YOU WERE ALL RIGHT--

I'M *FINE*, MACEY.
SORRY TO WORRY YOU.

sigh

YOU KNOW, I UNDERSTAND I AM NOT REALLY YOUR BIG SISTER, OR YOUR LEGAL GUARDIAN, BUT--I WOULD HOPE BY NOW YOU FEEL LIKE YOU CAN TALK TO ME AS THOUGH I AM--
WHO KNOWS, IT MIGHT MAKE ME BETTER AT THIS WHOLE 'COVER IDENTITY' THING.
YOU ARE PRETTY TERRIBLE AT IT.

HA, HA. SO COME ON, THEN--YOUNG GUILLAUME MISSES HIS FRIENDS FROM THE CAMP?
MM--
MY PSYCHIC POWERS TELL ME ONE IN PARTICULAR... LET'S SEE...

...SO, COME ON THEN, NO USE HIDING IT, WHICH ONE? YOU KNOW I'LL BE ABLE TO TELL--
TELL ME!
GO AWAY! NO!

IF I TELL YOU, DO YOU PROMISE TO GO TO BED AND STOP BUGGING ME?
IT'S A DEAL. NOW REVEAL THE SECRET LOVE THAT HAUNTS YOUR DREAMS TO ME!

HIM.

MM...AND WHO IS THIS, THEN? WILL I APPROVE OF HIM?
HIS NAME IS HISAO. AND HE'S THE BRAVEST, SMARTEST, KINDEST PERSON I'VE EVER KNOWN.

I SEE...
AND NOW I'LL NEVER SEE HIM AGAIN.
OF COURSE YOU WILL.

I'M NOT A LITTLE KID ANYMORE, MACEY. I KNOW WE'RE GOING TO DIE THERE. IN THAT PLACE WE'RE BEING SENT TO.
I'M JUST GLAD THEY DIDN'T MAKE HIM COME, TOO.

GUILLAUME, I HAVEN'T SEEN ALL THE THINGS YOU'VE SEEN... I DON'T HAVE WHAT YOU HAVE INSIDE YOU, BUT--
--THOSE OF US WHO WERE ASKED BY ABRAHAM TO WATCH OVER YOU AND YOUR FRIENDS, BEFORE YOU GO TO THIS SCHOOL--WE AGREED TO DO SO, BECAUSE WE BELIEVE IN YOU. WE HAVE FAITH IN YOU.
WHAT I'M TRYING TO SAY IS, I WOULD NEVER HAVE SAID YES IF I BELIEVED I WAS JUST HELPING TO SEND LAMBS OFF TO SLAUGHTER.
I BELIEVE YOU CAN OVERCOME THIS EVIL. THAT YOU--AND ALL OF US--WILL TRIUMPH IN THE END.

SO WHEN YOU ARE THERE, HOLD ON TO THIS HOPE. HOLD ON TO YOUR LOVE. AND I PROMISE YOU, NO MATTER WHAT HAPPENS--

NOW.
"--YOU WILL SURVIVE."
MGA

EXIT

WHAT HAPPENED TO YOU OUT THERE, GUILLAUME?
I MUST SAY, I AM HIGHLY DISAPPOINTED IN YOU. ON ONE LEVEL TOO MANY.
FIRST, YOU BETRAY THIS INSTITUTION AND ALL IT STANDS FOR--YOU AID THAT SICK LITTLE CUNT, IRINA, IN HER TRANSGRESSIONS AGAINST ALL THAT IS HOLY--
"--TRANSGRESSIONS THAT LEFT ONE OF OUR MOST BELOVED STUDENTS DEAD."
AND THEN, WHEN THE MAN WHO RUNS THIS PLACE, IN HIS INFINITE MERCY, SPARES YOU PUNISHMENT--
--A VERDICT, I CAN ASSURE YOU, I ARGUED MIGHTILY AGAINST--
--YOU RETURN HERE UNFOCUSED, UNPREPARED, AND DISTRACTED. SOFT.
PATHETIC.

I'LL NOT BE HERE MUCH LONGER--I'VE ASKED FOR A SABBATICAL, TO ATTEND TO BUSINESS AWAY FROM THIS CAMPUS--
--BUT BEFORE I GO, I HAVE THIS MATTER OF THE RED CAPTAIN'S TRYOUTS TO DECIDE.

AND SO I SHOULD THANK YOU, FOR THE MOCKERY OF THE SPORT YOU MADE TODAY.
IT GAVE ME A WONDERFUL IDEA.

FOR THE ARROGANCE YOU SHOWED IN SEEKING SUCH A COVETED POSITION...AND THE ABSOLUTE INEPTITUDE WITH WHICH YOU FOLLOWED UP THAT HUBRIS...I HAVE A REWARD.
YOU WILL BE A CAPTAIN, AFTER ALL, SOREL--

--OF THE BLUE TEAM.

R.GRIBBS
BLAM!

HEY, GUILLAUME!
BETTER FUTU
HUNTER, NOT NOW, MY FRIEND--
WHAT? I JUST WANNA KNOW HOW IT WENT--
PISS OFF!

UM--I JUST ASKED A STUPID QUESTION, DIDN'T I?
URE
IT IS NOT YOUR FAULT. WORD HAS ALREADY TRAVELED--
--GUILLAUME HAS BEEN MADE CAPTAIN OF THE BLUE TEAM.

BUT I DON'T GET IT--
--I THOUGHT HE WAS TRYING OUT TO BE A CAPTAIN? ISN'T THAT A GOOD THING?
NO, IT IS NOT. NOT AT ALL.
MAN, I JUST DO NOT GET SPORTS.
sigh
I WILL EXPLAIN--

"--IN TOWERBALL, THERE ARE ONLY TWO TEAMS. THE RED AND THE BLUE. THEY PLAY ONE SERIES, WITH WHOEVER WINS TWO GAMES OF A POSSIBLE THREE BEING DECLARED THE VICTOR. NOTHING SO UNUSUAL THERE--
"--EXCEPT THAT, BEFORE THE FIRST-EVER MATCHES, THE HEADMASTER DECLARED THAT ONLY RED WOULD EVER WIN THE SERIES--

"--AND SO IT HAS BEEN, EVERY YEAR, BLUE IS DEFEATED."
"SO THEY THROW THE GAMES?"
"TO THE CONTRARY-- THE BLUE TEAM ALWAYS GIVES THEIR BEST EFFORT. OTHERWISE, THE PUNISHMENT FROM THE COACHES WOULD BE SEVERE."

SO ARE THEY JUST SHITTIER PLAYERS, THEN? LIKE, WOULD I BE ON THE BLUE TEAM?
NO, IN FACT SOME YEARS, THE BLUE TEAM IS MUCH MORE TALENTED--

"--BUT NO MATTER WHAT, SOMETHING ALWAYS HAPPENS--
"--AN INJURY, A FREAK PLAY--THE OUTCOME IS ALWAYS THE SAME. WHICH IS EXACTLY THE MESSAGE THE ACADEMY WISHES TO IMPART."

"SO OF COURSE, THE TRUE COMPETITION AMONG THE PLAYERS IS TO BECOME THE RED CAPTAIN--
"--THE ONE PLAYER WHO CAN ALWAYS BE ASSURED OF NEVER ENDING UP ON THE BLUE TEAM, AND THE PLAYER WHO CAN SELECT HIS TEAMMATES, WHICH GIVES THEM CONSIDERABLE INFLUENCE ON CAMPUS.
"GUILLAUME IS A FIERCE COMPETITOR, AND ONE OF THE STAR PLAYERS.
"HE'S BEEN ON THE RED TEAM, BUT HE'S NEVER BEEN A CAPTAIN. MANY THOUGHT, HOWEVER, THAT THIS WOULD BE HIS SEASON--
"--GIVEN THE LAST CAPTAIN--HISAO FUKAYAMA--IS NO LONGER HERE TO PROTECT HIS TITLE."
FUTURE
OH. HIM, HUH? CRAZY...
...YOU KNOW, HOW HE'S NOT ALIVE ANYMORE.
I MEAN, DEAD.

MAINTENANCE

SO?

IT *WORKED.*

YOU'RE OFFICIALLY LOOKING AT THE CAPTAIN OF THE BLUE TEAM.
I STILL DON'T UNDERSTAND WHY THIS IS A GOOD THING--
YOU STILL DON'T GET THIS, DUMMY?

BECAUSE OF YOU.

YOU ARE THE BEST PLAYER I'VE EVER COMPETED AGAINST--
WE DIDN'T COMPETE. I WON.
sigh
FINE. EVEN BETTER THAN ME. AT LEAST, BACK THEN.
BUT THAT ISN'T THE POINT--

--EVERY YEAR, BLUE LOSES, ONE WAY OR ANOTHER, YES? WE ALL KNOW THIS.
BUT THIS YEAR, WE KNOW SOMETHING ELSE--SOMETHING THE HEADMASTER DOESN'T KNOW--
--YOU'RE YOU.

EVERYONE HERE THINKS YOU'RE HISAO. OR--JUN. IT'S A MESS, BUT, THE POINT REMAINS--
--THEY BELIEVE YOU ARE YOUR BROTHER, AND THAT YOU ARE DEAD.
SO?

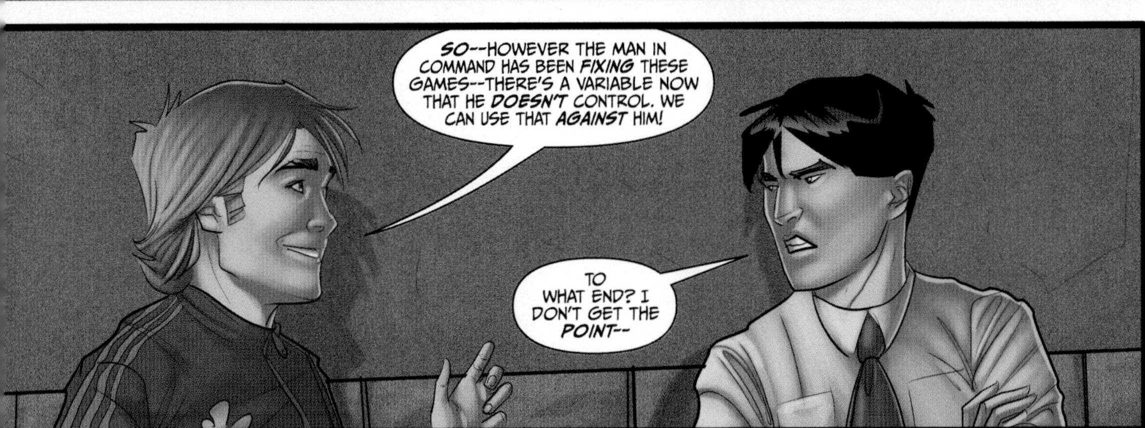
SO--HOWEVER THE MAN IN COMMAND HAS BEEN FIXING THESE GAMES--THERE'S A VARIABLE NOW THAT HE DOESN'T CONTROL. WE CAN USE THAT AGAINST HIM!
TO WHAT END? I DON'T GET THE POINT--

DON'T YOU SEE? IF BLUE WINS, IT WILL SEND A MESSAGE TO THE STUDENTS--HEADMASTER CAN BE WRONG. HIS WORD IS NOT LAW.
IT WILL SHOW THEM THAT HE CAN BE DEFIED--AND BEATEN. THAT WE BEAT HIM.

...SO WHAT DO I HAVE TO DO?
WELL...YOU'RE NOT GOING TO LIKE THIS PART. THAT GAME YOU'RE SO GOOD AT, THE ONE YOU WON ALL THOSE TROPHIES FOR?

I NEED YOU TO SUCK AT IT.

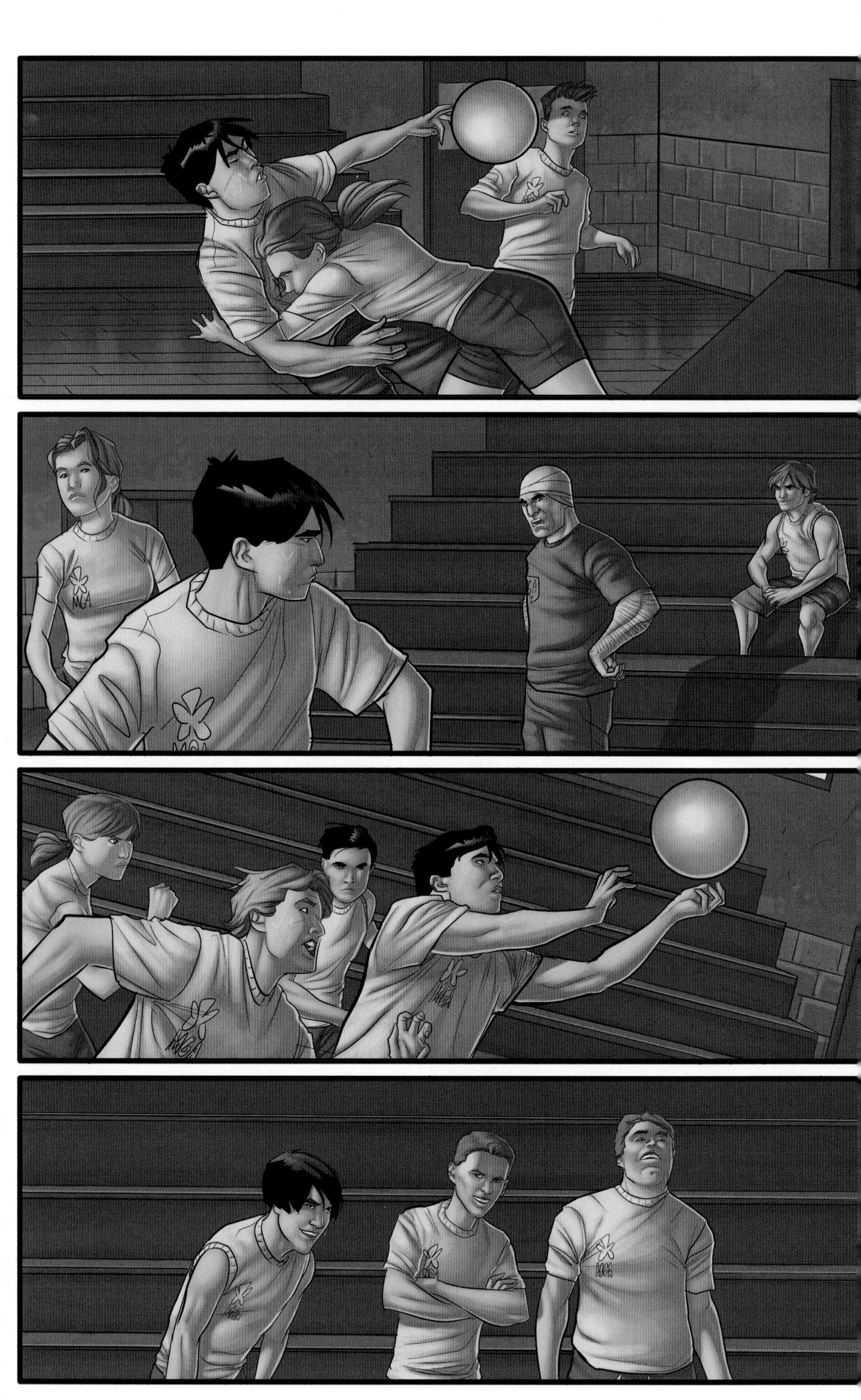

WELCOME, WELCOME, STUDENT ATHLETES! TODAY IS FIRST ROUND SELECTION DAY--
MEANING SIX LUCKY PLAYERS ARE ABOUT TO FIND OUT WHAT TEAM THEY STAND WITH IN THIS YEAR'S TOWERBALL FACE-OFF!
THESE PLAYERS--ONE FOR OFFENSE, ONE FOR DEFENSE, AND ONE FOR SPECIAL TEAMS, WILL THEN CONSULT WITH THEIR CAPTAINS, AND RETURN NEXT WEEK, TO CHOOSE THE REST OF THEIR PLAYERS!

REMEMBER, WHETHER YOU'RE CHOSEN OR NOT, EVERYONE IS A WINNER--

EXCEPT THE STUPID BLUE TEAM! GOOOO RED TEAM!
BLUE TEAM DIES IN A FIRE WITH THEIR MOMMY LAUGHING AT THEM THE WHOLE TIME!
BLUE TEAM'S DIRTY PARTS TURN GREEN THEN FALL OFF!

BLUE TEAM'S KITTEN GETS DROWNED IN A GARBAGE BAG!
YOU SUCK, BLUE TEAM!
ER--YES.
SOREL--YOU HAVE THE FIRST SELECTION.

DENISE.
FUCK.

THANKS A LOT, ASSHOLE.
KELLI?
JOSH.

GUILLAUME?

TOBY.
WHY *ME*, GOD?

AND KELLI--
ANASTASIA.
GOOD, THEN--

AND NOW FOR THE FINAL SELECTIONS...
...SOREL?

WE NEED SOMEONE FOR OFFENSE--
GO WITH LONNIE, OR WILL--
JUN.

DUDE, WHAT ARE YOU DOING?
HE SUCKS!

EHH...GUILLAUME--MIGHT I REMIND YOU, YOU ARE HONOR BOUND TO COMPETE TO THE BEST OF YOUR ABILITY--
I'M WELL AWARE OF THAT, COACH.
THEN, PERHAPS WE DIDN'T HEAR YOU CORRECTLY, AND YOU'D LIKE TO SPEAK YOUR CHOICE AGAIN, BOY?
OF COURSE, BUT I BELIEVE YOU HEARD ME WELL--

--I SELECT JUN FUKAYAMA.

AND YOU SHOULD HAVE **SEEN** THEIR FACES-- THEY HAVE **NO** IDEA WHAT'S GOING ON!

YOU ALWAYS **WERE** GOOD AT PRANKS.
MAYBE I JUST LIKED GETTING **ATTENTION** FROM YOU.
AND **YOU** WERE ALWAYS AN EASY **MARK**.
AH, SO **NOW** WHO WAS THE FOOL!

THE SUN IS TOO **BRIGHT**--
WE'RE NOT SUPPOSED TO SEE THE FACE OF GOD, MY LOVE. LOOK AWAY.
LIKE ALL THINGS--

--IT WILL PASS.

GUILLAUME.

GUILLAUME, WAKE *UP.*

JUN? WHAT ARE YOU--
SSH--I WANT YOU TO COME WITH ME.
WHY? WHAT *IS* THIS?

I HAVE HELPED YOU WITH *YOUR* SILLY LITTLE GAME.
NOW YOU WILL HELP *ME.*

WHERE ARE WE GOING? THIS PLACE--
HAS BEEN CLOSED OFF TO EVERYONE SINCE THE INSURRECTION.
STRUCTURAL DAMAGE.
WHICH IS WHY NO ONE WILL THINK TO LOOK HERE.
KEEPOUT//KEEP

LOOK HERE FOR WHAT?
THIS IS WHERE IT HAPPENED. WHERE HE SACRIFICED HIMSELF FOR ME--FOR ALL OF US. BUT I WAS ALWAYS TAUGHT THIS PLACE WAS HOLY--SACRED.
YOUR TEACHER, THE MAN THEY CALL ABRAHAM--
--HE BELIEVED THESE THINGS AS WELL--

--NOW WE WILL PUT IT TO THE TEST.
OH GOD... NO...

THEY SAY A SACRIFICE IS ALWAYS DEMANDED, DON'T THEY?
WELL, THIS IS MY DEMAND.
JUN... WHAT IS THIS? WHAT--
--WHAT ARE YOU DOING DOWN HERE?
WHAT ARE WE DOING--

--BRINGING MY BROTHER BACK TO LIFE.

fortytwo

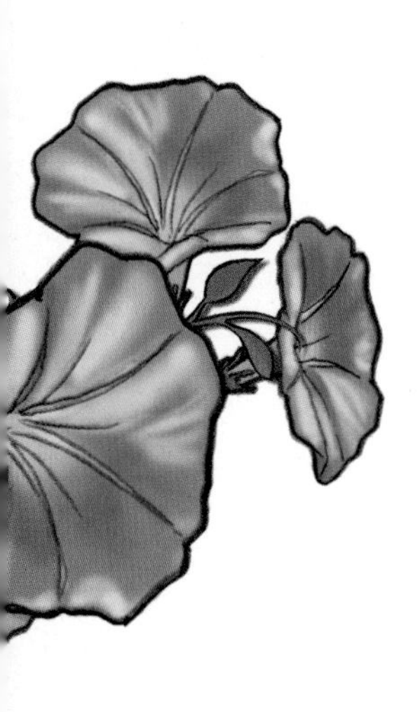
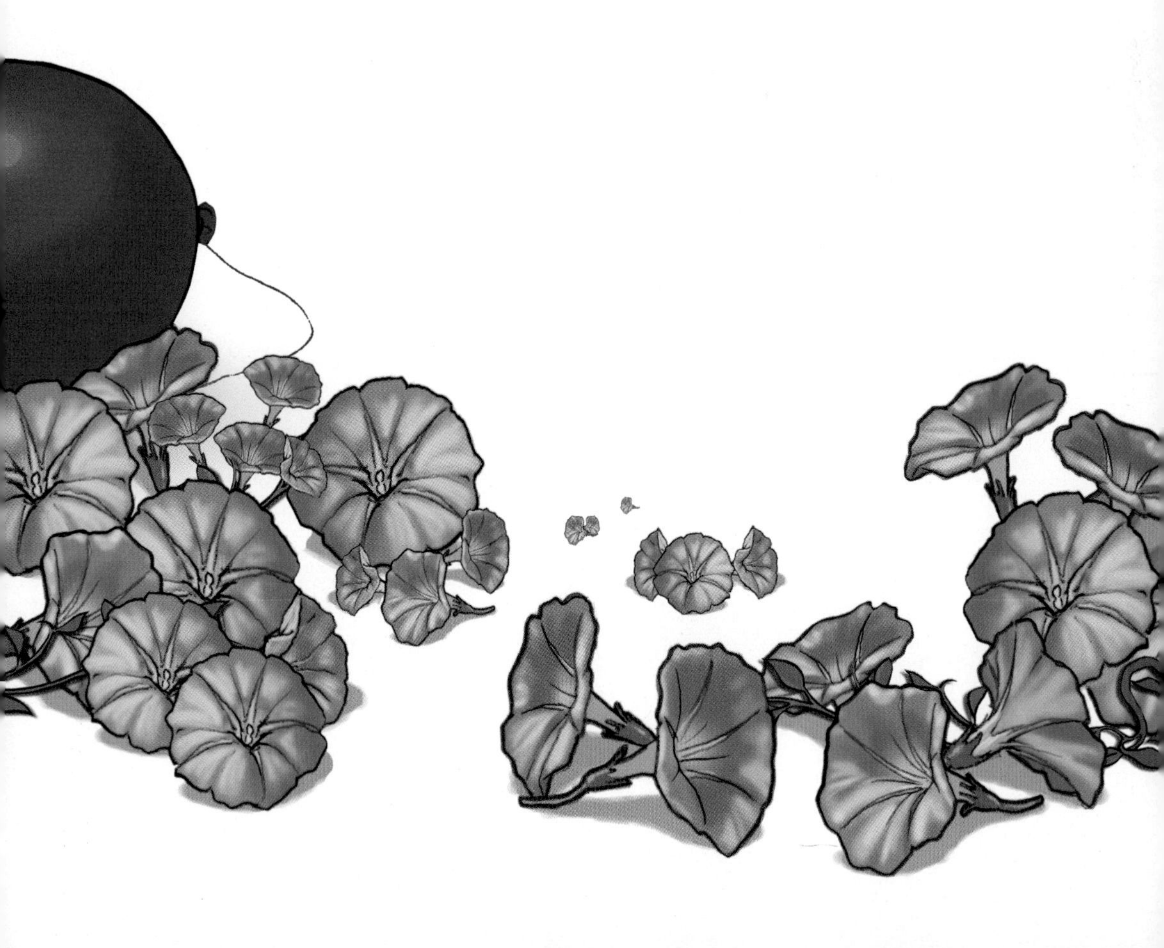

MGA

MY CHEMICAL ROMANCE
OH, WONDERFUL, *THERE* SHE IS.
JUST IN TIME, DEAR--
LIBRARY
I'M SO *GLAD* YOU GOT MY MESSAGE.

AW, NO...
WHAT'S WRONG, CHILD?

WHAT'S WRONG? I'M HAVING THESE STUPID FUCKING DREAMS AGAIN!
WELL, YOU CAN'T VERY WELL UNDERSTAND WHERE YOU'RE GOING UNLESS YOU KNOW WHERE YOU'VE BEEN.
OH, I BET THAT'LL MAKE SENSE SOMEDAY! THANKS A WHOLE SHITTING LOT!
TAKE ME, FOR INSTANCE--

--I HELD THE BLADE TO HIS LITTLE THROAT AND I KNEW--I KNEW WHAT I WAS SUPPOSED TO DO, BUT--
--I HAVE HATED MYSELF EVER SINCE.

WHOA, HEY, JUST, UH, PUT THE KNIFE DOWN, OKAY? I MEAN, I GET THIS ISN'T REAL, OR IT MIGHT BE LATER, OR WHATEVER, BUT--
--DON'T DO IT.
I LOVED HIM THE INSTANT I SAW HIM.

EVEN THOUGH I KNEW WHAT HE WAS.
WHAT HE WOULD DO TO US.

THE HOUR OF OUR RELEASE DRAWS NEAR
YOU HAVE TO STOP HER, SISTER--

THEY'RE SETTING A TRAP FOR HER. YOU CAN'T LET HER GO IN.
GO IN WHERE?

SHE'S NOT READY. EVERYONE WILL DIE.

EVERYONE? I GOTTA GO TELL--
EEE!
SHH!

DO NOT SCREAM.

THE NEXT MORNING.

Marines

Marines

Marines
JADE?

I'M GONNA ASK YOU ONE MORE TIME...
WHERE IS SHE?!!!
OOF.

CASEY, IT'S EARLY.
YOU GOTTA AT LEAST GIVE ME SOME KIND OF HINT--
DON'T EVEN START TO PRETEND LIKE YOU DON'T KNOW WHAT I'M TALKING ABOUT.

JADE'S GONE.
WAIT-- WHAT?

SHE'S GONE.
WHAT DO YOU MEAN, GONE? HAVE YOU CHECKED AROUND?
DID YOU HEAR WHAT I JUST SAID? DON'T ACT LIKE YOU AREN'T IN ON THIS--
ARE YOU SURE SHE DIDN'T SNEAK OFF SOMEWHERE?
MAYBE FOUND A QUIET SPOT PERFECT FOR WRITING TERRIBLE POETRY?

ENOUGH! LOOK, I DON'T EVEN CARE WHAT KIND OF BULLSHIT GAME YOU'RE PLAYING--
--BUT IF YOU EXPECT ME TO BELIEVE THAT, NOT LONG AFTER YOU COME TO ME AND TRY TO GET ME TO RUN IN YOUR STUPID STUDENT COUNCIL ELECTIONS, MY ROOMMATE DISAPPEARS, AND YOU HAD NOTHING TO DO WITH IT--

--LET'S JUST SKIP TO THE PART WHERE I FIND HER AND BRING HER BACK WHILE MAKING YOU ALL LOOK LIKE ASSHOLES.
BECAUSE WE HAVE DEFINITELY BEEN DOWN THIS ROAD BEFORE.

ƸsighƸ
CASEY, FIRST OF ALL, NOT THAT I EXPECT YOU TO TRUST ME, BUT--
--WHILE I WILL ADMIT I WAS HALF ASLEEP DURING THE BREAKFAST MEETING OF THE NEFARIOUS OVERLORDS THAT RUN THIS PLACE, I DO NOT RECALL HEARING ABOUT ANY PLANS TO IMPRISON OR KIDNAP YOUR LITTLE FRECKLED FRIEND.
WELL--
--NO MORE THAN WE ALREADY HAVE, I GUESS.
THAT SAID--

--IF YOU DID FOLLOW MY EARLIER ADVICE REGARDING OUR ELECTIONS, AND ALL TURNED OUT AS I BELIEVE IT WOULD, YOU WOULD BE ABLE TO ASK THESE QUESTIONS TO SOMEONE CAPABLE OF GIVING A MUCH MORE INFORMED ANSWER THAN I COULD EVER HOPE TO--SOMEONE WHO COULD ANSWER ANY OF YOUR QUESTIONS--
--ALL OF THEM, IN FACT, AND NOT ONLY THAT, BUT COULD PROVIDE YOU WITH SOLUTIONS TO PROBLEMS LIKE THESE.
MIGHT CUT DOWN ON THE THEATRICS AROUND HERE QUITE A BIT IS ALL I'M SAYING.

SO THAT IS WHAT THIS IS.
YOU TAKE HER, GET ME TO RUN SO THAT I CAN FIND OUT WHERE SHE IS--
NO, NO, NO. ONE OF THESE IS NOT LIKE THE OTHER.
NO ONE IS TRYING TO TRICK YOU INTO DOING THE RIGHT THING. THIS IS YOUR CHOICE.
FRANKLY, CASEY, I GET YOU'RE USED TO THE SOFT SELL WITH ME, BUT IF I WANTED TO FORCE YOU INTO DOING THIS--

--THEN I WOULD JUST FUCKING DO IT, LITTLE GIRL.

NOW, AS TO THE MATTER AT HAND, I DO WANT TO HELP.
I'LL ALERT SECURITY IMMEDIATELY--WE'LL DO EVERYTHING WE CAN TO FIND HER.
GO GREEN!
IN THE MEANTIME, THOUGH, I WOULDN'T WORRY TOO MUCH.
I HAVE A GOOD SENSE OF THESE THINGS, AND WHEREVER SHE IS--

"--I'M SURE SHE'S *FINE.*"

THIS IS CRAZY!
THIS IS THE ONLY WAY. YOU ***KNOW*** THAT.

WE CAN BRING MY BROTHER ***BACK--***
NO, IDIOT, WE CAN'T--
WE CAN MAKE IT SO HE NEVER ***DIED!***
THE ***THINGS*** WE CAN DO--

THE THINGS I CAN DO, YOU MEAN. THE THINGS HE COULD DO--YOU, ON THE OTHER HAND--
THAT MAY HAVE BEEN TRUE BEFORE. BUT I AM IN HIS BODY NOW, REMEMBER?
AND THE CEREMONY ONLY REQUIRES TWO OF US--
AND A SACRIFICE!
WE CAN'T JUST KILL SOMEONE--

WHO IS SHE TO YOU?
YOU WERE MORE THAN WILLING TO TAKE MY LIFE TO HELP THAT BITCH IRINA WITH HER FAILED REVOLUTION.
IT WAS FINE THEN, BUT NOT NOW? NOT FOR HISAO?!!
YOU SAID YOU LOVED MY BROTHER--

--APPARENTLY NOT VERY MUCH.

SLAM!

DON'T YOU **EVER** QUESTION MY LOVE FOR HIM, YOU PATHETIC, BRAINWASHED **FUCK!** IT WAS **YOU** HE DIED TRYING TO SAVE, **REMEMBER?**
YOU'RE RIGHT, I **DIDN'T** CARE, BECAUSE I KNEW WHAT A SICK **ASSHOLE** YOU WERE--
--AND NOW YOU WANT ME TO KILL AN INNOCENT **GIRL?!**

unff
YOU THINK I CHOSE THIS **LIGHTLY?!!** YOU THINK **I** CHOSE HER.
HERE-- SEE FOR **YOURSELF**--

IT'S ALL IN HER FILE. SHE ISN'T ONE OF **US.**
READ IT--

--YOU'LL **SEE** WHY IT SHOULD BE HER.

IKE!
OH, MY MISTRESS! HER VOICE!

AND AFTER BEING IGNORED FOR SO LONG--
TRUST ME, I WOULDN'T BE SPEAKING TO YOU IF I DIDN'T HAVE TO.
I UNDERSTAND. IT'S LIKE A MAGNETIC PULL--YOU FOUGHT AS LONG AS YOU COULD.
YOUR FAVORITE STALL GLORYHOLE OR MINE?

CHRIST--YOU KNOW, I TELL HER TO STAY AWAY FROM YOU, BUT FOR WHATEVER REASON, SHE APPARENTLY REFUSES TO SEE YOU FOR THE SAD, TWISTED PIECE OF SHIT YOU ARE...
...STILL, MAYBE IT CAN AT LEAST COME IN HANDY FOR ONCE...
I'M AFRAID I DON'T FOLLOW--

JADE'S MISSING.
WHAT?
I THINK-- I THINK THEY MAY HAVE TAKEN HER AGAIN.

DAMN IT...
SO IF YOU KNOW ANYTHING, THAT COULD HELP US--
THAT MIGHT DEPEND--

--WHICH ONE IS JADE AGAIN?

YOU SON OF A BITCH...
CASEY, WAIT--

WELL, IF YOU CHANGE YOUR MIND, IT'S STALL THREE OF THE CAFETERIA MEN'S!
ER, STALL TWO FOR YOU.

LAUGH IT UP, ASSHOLE. BUT I'D BE WILLING TO BET THAT GIRL IS THE ONLY REAL FRIEND YOU'VE EVER HAD.
AND SOONER OR LATER--

"--WE ALL NEED FRIENDS."
SHE'S BEEN GONE HOW LONG?
JUST THIS MORNING, I KNOW--BUT TRUST ME, CASEY WOULDN'T BE ASKING AROUND IF IT WASN'T FOR REAL--

THIS IS THE GIRL THEY TOOK TO NINE WHEN YOU ARRIVED?
YEAH--JADE. SHE'S COOL. I MEAN, KINDA CREEPY-GOTHY OR WHATEVER, AND SHE'S ALWAYS CRYING, BUT--
--SHE'S COOL.
SOUNDS LIKE IT.

I'M JUST SAYING--WE COULD USE THE ANSWER TO HELP FIND HER. PUT THE WORD OUT, ASK IF ANYONE'S SEEN HER.
AND IF THEY HAVE? WHAT THEN?
WELL, I WAS THINKING ABOUT THAT, TOO--

--I FIGURE WE NEED SOME KIND OF 'TIP JAR.' YOU KNOW, LIKE NOT FOR MONEY, BUT FOR NEWS TIPS.
YEAH, WE GOT THAT.
SO PEOPLE COULD GIVE US A HEAD'S UP ON THINGS, BE OUR SOURCES--

IT IS A GOOD IDEA, HUNTER, BUT... THERE WOULD BE RISKS.
SHE'S RIGHT. AS OF NOW, THE FACULTY HAVE NO WAY OF TYING THE ANSWER BACK TO US. BUT WHEREVER WE PUT THIS...
...TIP JAR, THEY COULD MOST CERTAINLY PLACE SURVEILLANCE ON IT.
SET A TRAP WHEN WE COME FOR IT.
I THOUGHT ABOUT THAT, TOO!
BUT WHAT IF WE PUT IT SOMEWHERE NO ONE COULD GET TO--
--AT LEAST NOT WHEN THEY'RE AWAKE.
DO YOU MEAN...
IT COULD WORK.
YEAH, IT COULD!
I'LL ADMIT, IT'S GOT POTENTIAL.
WE SHOULD TALK TO IAN ABOUT IT.
A BRILLIANT IDEA, HUNTER--
OH, COME ON!
LOOK, I GET YOU GUYS ARE FRIENDS, AND I'M NEW AND ALL-- AND YEAH, HIS FORTUNATO STORY WAS REALLY GOOD, AND HE LISTENED TO ME ABOUT THAT, BUT...
STILL...
DON'T YOU EVER FEEL LIKE HE'S--
I DUNNO...

"--A LITTLE OFF?"
AH, IAN--NOT TO BE A BUZZKILL, BUT I'M NOT ENTIRELY CERTAIN THIS IS ALLOWED...
AND I SAY THAT'S YOUR DECISION TO MAKE, DADDY DEAREST. AFTER ALL, THEY GAVE YOU KEYS, DIDN'T THEY?
THAT MEANS YOU'RE THEY NOW, TOO.
HARDLY. I AM INTERIM FACULTY. EMPHASIS UPON THE INTERIM.
AND WHILE WE HAVE NO WAY OF KNOWING JUST WHAT THESE VIOLENT FANATICS INTEND TO DO WITH ME ONCE I'VE SERVED MY PURPOSE HERE...
...IF IT'S ALL RIGHT BY YOU, I'D MUCH PREFER IT INVOLVE ME STILL BEING ALIVE!
I DON'T THINK YOU QUITE UNDERSTAND HOW THIS FEELS FOR ME--BEING POKED AND PRODDED...A RAT IN THEIR MAZE...
YES, FATHER. I ACTUALLY AM SOMEWHAT FAMILIAR WITH THE FEELING.
ER, YES-- I JUST--I DON'T EVEN UNDERSTAND WHAT YOU NEED WITH THIS TO BEGIN WITH.
SUCH AN ANTIQUATED PIECE OF TECHNOLOGY...
AND I ALREADY EXPLAINED IT TO YOU--

--IT'S FOR MY SCIENCE PROJECT.

AND THEN THE MOONCHILD LUMBERS OVER--SUTTON JUST HAS THIS BLANK EXPRESSION AND HE SAYS, 'THAT'S GOOD. I'M ACTUALLY NOT SCARED, DES. I'M NOT. SEE...'
'...I THINK IT LIKES ME.'

I DON'T KNOW IF I'M *TELLING* IT RIGHT--READING COMICS TO SOMEONE IS WEIRDLY *DIFFICULT,* ACTUALLY.
IT IS A VERY GOOD STORY, AKIKO.
I *KNOW,* RIGHT? MORRISON'S LIKE A *GOD.* THE FIRST TIME I READ THIS ONE I COULDN'T SLEEP ALL *NIGHT.* AND YET--

--YOU COME OFF A LITTLE *DISTRACTED,* FORTUNATO.
I AM SORRY.
THIS IS ABOUT *IAN,* ISN'T IT?
I REALLY WISH YOU WOULD TELL ME WHAT HE SAID.

I--I CAN'T...
WHY *NOT?!!* I *KNOW* HE WAS A DICK TO YOU--
--UHNN, I AM *SO* MAD AT THAT JERK!
NO...HE IS *YOUR* BEST FRIEND. AND A BROTHER TO *US.*

I GET IT, I JUST--I DON'T KNOW WHAT TO DO.
HE NEEDS ME, YOU KNOW? HE'S NO GOOD WHEN HE'S LEFT ALONE. HE GETS...WEIRD.
I MEAN... MORE WEIRD THAN USUAL.
I TRIED TO TALK TO HIM, BUT-- HE'S LIKE EVERYONE ELSE. HE CAN'T HEAR ME--

--NOBODY BUT YOU CAN HEAR ME.
AKIKO...

...READ ME MORE OF YOUR STORY.
OH... OH, SURE.
THE NEXT ONE'S MY FAVORITE-- WELL, MY SECOND FAVORITE, TO THE LAST ONE--

--IT'S ABOUT ONE OF THOSE NAMELESS GUARDS WE SAW KING MOB KILL BEFORE--
--IT'S ALL ABOUT BEFORE HE DIED...

Dear Vanessa,
It pains me to have to write this, when you are so close I should just be able to look you in the eye, and speak to you. To be your mother again.

But the monsters who run this place have decided it's best we're kept separated, at least for now.
I can't say I'm surprised by their cruelty.

But I wanted you to know that I will find a way for us to be together again. To be a family again.
I have missed you for so long...

And there is so much I need to tell you.
I only wish we had more time.

GO RAMS

IT'S GOOD TO BE BACK ON *TOP.*
TRUE, MAYBE--

--THOUGH I IMAGINE IT VERY MUCH DEPENDS ON WHAT YOU'VE GOT HIDING *BELOW.*
sigh
HELLO, LARA. APOLOGIES IF YOU WERE WAITING IN THE DARK LONG, I DIDN'T SEE A DRAMATIC *ENTRANCE* ON MY SCHEDULE.

DON'T PLAY QUEEN BITCH WITH *ME,* GEORGINA. I'M NOT ONE OF THOSE *KIDS* OUT THERE. OR *ELSEWHERE,* FOR THAT MATTER.
SEE, THIS IS YOUR *PROBLEM,* DEAR.
I'VE HEARD YOUR CRYPTICISMS ENOUGH I CAN GENERALLY PIECE THEM *TOGETHER.*
THIS IS ABOUT FORTUNATO, *ISN'T* IT?
WELL, BEFORE YOU EVEN *BEGIN--*

--I'LL BE *RELEASING* HIM SOON, I HAVE NO *DESIRE* TO TEST FATHER'S PATIENCE. IT'S JUST, THE LONGER THEY GO WITHOUT *SEEING* HIM, THE MORE DELIGHTFUL THE STORY GETS-- DID YOU HEAR I BIT HIS *EARS* OFF AS WELL NOW?
BEEN *WONDERFUL* FOR RESTORING ORDER. AND THIS SCHOOL *NEWSPAPER!* WHAT A GIFT. THE YOUNG *DO* CRAVE AUTHENTICITY.

YOU--YOU'RE *SICK,* GEORGINA. THAT BOY WAS TO BE SPARED, JUST LIKE THE *REST* OF THEM--
AND HE *WAS.* I MERELY SOUGHT TO FIRST INSTILL IN HIM A VALUABLE *LESSON--*
--YOU *MAIMED* HIM!
I OFFERED TO LET YOU *HELP!*

YOU SEE, THIS IS OUR *PROBLEM,* LARA, WE DON'T DO THINGS TOGETHER AS *SISTERS* ANYMORE.
ENOUGH-- I'M NOT HERE ABOUT FORTUNATO ANYWAY, AND YOU *KNOW* IT--

WHERE'S JADE?

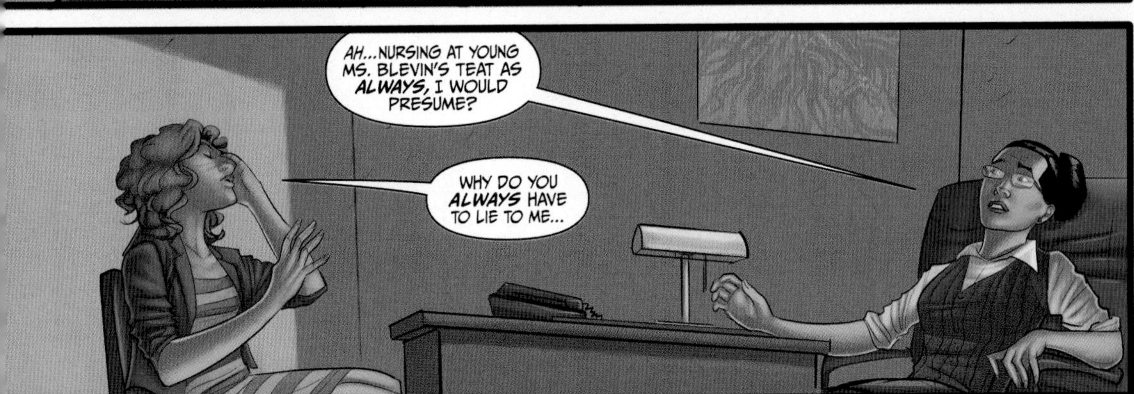
AH...NURSING AT YOUNG MS. BLEVIN'S TEAT AS ALWAYS, I WOULD PRESUME?
WHY DO YOU ALWAYS HAVE TO LIE TO ME...

LARA, I'M AFRAID I HAVE NO CLUE WHAT YOU MEAN--
I JUST COVERED FOR YOU WITH CASEY.
NOW'S THE PART WHERE YOU TELL ME WHAT'S GOING ON. WHERE WE WORK TOGETHER, SO I DON'T HAVE TO SWOOP IN AND SAVE YOU FROM YOUR OWN MESS.
AGAIN.
I HONESTLY DON'T UNDERSTAND THE NATURE OF THIS GAME...

FINE, SIS. WE DO IT YOUR WAY. PLAY YOUR GAMES.
FORGET ONCE AGAIN THAT, NO MATTER WHAT PROTECTION FATHER AFFORDS US, WE ARE STILL THEIR SERVANTS--NOT THEIR JAILERS. OR THEIR TORTURERS.
BUT I AM WARNING YOU, ONE LAST TIME--THERE IS A CHANGE COMING.
ALL OF THIS IS GOING TO END. IT'S INEVITABLE. AND WHEN IT DOES, WHAT THEY WILL DO TO YOU IN RETURN...

...THAT'S NOT SOMETHING EVEN I CAN SAVE YOU FROM.

BETTER
FUTURE

TELL ME WHAT TO DO...

"AND NOW, PLEASE JOIN ME IN WELCOMING BACK--YOUR STUDENT COUNCIL PRESIDENT--ISABEL TRAVEISO!"

THANK YOU, THANK YOU-- IT IS GOOD TO BE BACK.
CLAP CLAP CLAP CLAP CLAP CLAP CLAP CLAP CLAP CLAP
CLAP CLAP CLAP CLAP CLAP CLAP CLAP CLAP
"BACK WHERE I KNOW I BELONG--"

--BACK *HOME.*
NOW, I KNOW THAT MIGHT SOUND A LITTLE STRANGE TO SOME OF YOU, ESPECIALLY OUR *NEWER* CLASSMATES.
HOW COULD I EVER CALL THIS PLACE *HOME?*

"MANY OF US, *INCLUDING* MYSELF--WE WERE BROUGHT HERE AGAINST OUR WILL."
"TAKEN FROM OUR FRIENDS AND OUR FAMILIES."

AND WE DO MISS THEM. IN FAR TOO MANY CASES--
--WE MOURN THEM.

"SO HOW CAN I STILL CLAIM TO LOVE THIS PLACE, GIVEN ALL THE PAIN AND SUFFERING IT HAS CAUSED US?"
"WHY WOULD I SEEK TO SERVE THIS INSTITUTION, AND STRENGTHEN IT, RATHER THAN OPPOSE IT?"

AND THE ANSWER IS SIMPLE. IT'S BECAUSE I BELIEVE THAT ALL OF THIS HAS HAPPENED FOR A REASON.
I BELIEVE WE WERE BROUGHT HERE--FOR A PURPOSE.

"AND THAT PURPOSE IS GREATER THAN ME--GREATER THAN ALL OF US."
STUDENT COUNCIL ASSEMBLY

YES, WE ARE ASKED TO SACRIFICE. YES, WE ENDURE THINGS NO ONE SHOULD HAVE TO.
BUT THIS IS THE PRICE OF EDUCATION, OF INSTRUCTION--
--KNOWLEDGE OF THE TRUTH DOES NOT COME WITHOUT A PRICE.

"BUT WORKING IN UNITY WITH OUR TEACHERS, AND, MOST IMPORTANTLY, OUR BELOVED HEADMASTER, WE HAVE COME SO FAR.
"AND I KNOW WE CAN DO SO MUCH MORE, IF WE ONLY CONTINUE TO SEEK HIS WILL. WHAT WONDERS WE'LL ACCOMPLISH!"

THAT IS WHY I'M PROUD TO STAND BEFORE YOU TODAY AND ASK THAT YOU RE-ELECT ME AS PRESIDENT OF THE STUDENT COUNCIL AND THIS STUDENT BODY!
IT HAS BEEN MY HONOR TO SERVE AS YOUR LEADER SINCE THIS COUNCIL WAS FORMED. AND YOUR CONTINUED SUPPORT WHILE I HAVE BEEN AWAY HAS MEANT THE WORLD TO ME.
CLAP CLAP CLAP CLAP CLAP CLAP CLAP CLAP CLAP CLAP CLAP CLAP CLAP CLAP

NOW, I DON'T WANT YOU TO THINK I TAKE YOUR VOTES FOR GRANTED, JUST BECAUSE NO ONE HAS DECLARED AN OPPOSITION TO OUR TICKET.
THAT ONLY FURTHERS MY RESOLVE, KNOWING THAT ALL OF YOU STAND WITH ME--
--BUT MAYBE THEY DON'T.

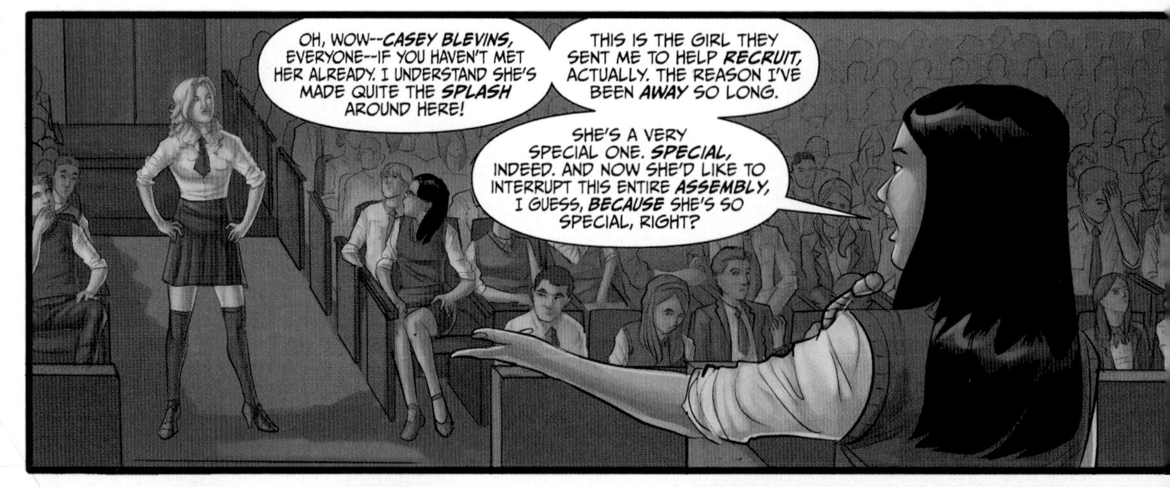
OH, WOW--CASEY BLEVINS, EVERYONE--IF YOU HAVEN'T MET HER ALREADY. I UNDERSTAND SHE'S MADE QUITE THE SPLASH AROUND HERE!
THIS IS THE GIRL THEY SENT ME TO HELP RECRUIT, ACTUALLY. THE REASON I'VE BEEN AWAY SO LONG.
SHE'S A VERY SPECIAL ONE. SPECIAL, INDEED. AND NOW SHE'D LIKE TO INTERRUPT THIS ENTIRE ASSEMBLY, I GUESS, BECAUSE SHE'S SO SPECIAL, RIGHT?

GO ON THEN, CASEY--
--YOU HAD SOMETHING YOU'D LIKE TO SHARE?
I WAS SAYING MAYBE THEY DON'T STAND WITH YOU. MAYBE THEY ACTUALLY CAN'T STAND YOU.
MAYBE THEY'RE JUST AFRAID OF YOU.
I SEE...

WELL, NOT YOU EXACTLY.
BUT THE PEOPLE YOU PLAY PUPPET FOR, I GUESS.
THE ONES WHO KIDNAPPED US, AND TORTURED US--
EXIT

--THE ONES WHO KILLED OUR FAMILIES.

CASEY, LOOK AROUND YOU--
--DO WE LOOK SCARED TO YOU?
MAYBE THEY'VE JUST BEEN PRETENDING FOR SO LONG, THEY'VE FORGOTTEN HOW MUCH THEY HATE YOU.
MAYBE YOU PLAY THE ACT FOR SO LONG IT STARTS TO FEEL REAL.

EITHER WAY, I THINK IF SOMEONE STOOD AGAINST YOU, YOU'D LOSE.
WELL, THAT JUST SHOWS HOW LITTLE RESPECT FOR WHAT WE'VE BUILT HERE--
OH, I AGREE.
I THINK THIS IS COMPLETE BULLSHIT, YOUR LITTLE SHAM STUDENT GOVERNMENT. IT'S PATHETIC, REALLY, PRETENDING WE WORK WITH THEM.
PRETENDING THIS PLACE IS ANYTHING BESIDES A PRISON.
MGA
EXIT

BUT THERE IS ONE THING THAT INTERESTS ME--THEY SAY WHOEVER GETS THE JOB CAN MEET WITH THIS HEADMASTER NO ONE EVER SHUTS UP ABOUT.
IT IS MY GREATEST HONOR IN LIFE...
I BET.
BUT I'D LIKE TO MEET WITH HIM, TOO.
DO YOU KNOW WHY, ISABEL?
MGA

BECAUSE THEN I WOULD KILL HIM.
I WOULD KILL HIM, AND TORCH THIS WHOLE GOD-FORSAKEN PLACE.

AND THEN WE WOULD ALL GO HOME.

MY, THAT'S QUITE A CAMPAIGN PROMISE. I MEAN, ASSUMING IT IS ONE...
DO YOU HAVE SOMETHING YOU'D LIKE TO ANNOUNCE THEN, CASEY?
I KNOW I FOR ONE CAN'T WAIT TO HEAR IT.

FUCK IT.

MGA
EXIT
MY NAME IS CASEY BLEVINS, AND I'M RUNNING FOR STUDENT COUNCIL PRESIDENT.
MGA
TO BE CONTINUED...

INSIDE THE ACADEMY

FEATURING MORNING GLORIES STUDY HALL WITH

MATTHEW MEYLIKHOV

Every issue of Morning Glories includes an in-depth examination of the events that transpired within the story by expert analyst, Matthew Meylikhov. What follows is the "Study Hall" entry for Issue #41 and a gallery of Morning Glories Babies strips scripted by Matt and illustrated by artist, Joe Eisma.

Hello.

My name is Professor Matthew Meylikhov. I'm here to help you with your reading of "Morning Glories" by looking at a few elements of the issue you should be aware of, courtesy of Multiversity Comics. I should note however that these are all based on theories I've personally developed-- and should not be taken as confirmed or endorsed by the creative team behind the book.

Let's begin, shall we?

TOWERBALL
Rodin Esquejo

MEET THE FOSTERS

One thing we learn right at the beginning of t issue when Guillaume talks to his step sist Macey (named after and resembling the real li "Morning Glories" superfan and runner of the M TinyChat Macey) is that the foster families are " on it" with Abraham. It'd been up for deba before as to what form of role they played Abraham's plan, whether they were unwitti participants or active members, but now i become a bit more clear: they're aware of t situation.

It's an interesting development, because we st know so very little about what most of the ki were up to when they left Abraham's camp. W know what happened to Zoe and Hisao throu flashbacks, but none of the Truants have shown what their family life was like – or if they ev really had one. Guillaume is incredibly cand with Macey, suggesting a certain amount knowledge passed between them, but Macey al doesn't seem aware of what Guillaume's tria entail in any specific way. It would seem that t foster families that Abraham reaches out to a given as little information as we are, most likely protect them given what happens to Irin "parents" in issue #21.

Still, we're slowly seeing that Abraham's netwo is much larger than we realized. Where t Academy seems like a focused front with eve member of their team centralized mostly to t school (despite occasionally going off campu Abraham's agents exist all around the world sleeper cells. It's interesting to see how the t players in this battle interact in that capacity, h they use the tools available to them, and i interesting to ruminate on what their use of ass says about each of them.

THE WORD OF GOD

In this issue we learn all about Towerball, game which I imagine many fans of the series a going to attempt to learn how to play in time hold a tournament at a comic convention. A while we won't get into that aspect of it here, o important aspect of Towerball is that all the gam are fixed for one team because the Headmast says so – and Guillaume, with help from Jun, wa to prove that this is something that can overthrown.

This is an interesting aspect of the game becau if we consider the infinite and almighty power the Headmaster, we can see his decree in paral with a lot of the parables about God that ha been featured throughout the series – specifical in regards to the role of God telling someone to

›mething and them being forced to do it without ‹estion. It's a frequently recurring aspect of the ›ries, something that became particularly prevalent hen the Truants entered into the scene and a lot of the eological aspects of the book went into overdrive, ıt the logic we have for God is that He is infallible and .n not be proven otherwise – so to do so would herently lead to potential disaster.

ıe question then becomes, if the Headmaster is our ıalogue for God on the school campus, what exactly ıppens if we prove him wrong? Theories exist about ıat the consequences would be to prove God wrong, ıe possible outcome and the most relevant would be e destruction of reality; if God created reality in his fallible image and we prove this to be a fallible ›ncept, it destroys the logic and reason that went into eation and therefore unwinds creation as a construct ›elf (something that would go very well with the scussion held in issue #40).

hile Guillaume suggests that this is to send a essage, it's actually also quite possible that proving e Headmaster wrong could have larger ramifications ›pending how omniscient the Headmaster truly is ıd how the reality of Morning Glory Academy is ›fined in conjunction with that. It's also interesting to ›te that we now have two separate parties actively ›ing something to put them in the crosshairs of the ›admaster, as Casey will be running for class esident specifically to meet him.

IT'S NOT A FASHION STATEMENT, IT'S A DEATHWISH

Of course, in helping Guillaume with the Towerball ›t, Jun wants something in return -- and, as we learn, ıt something is to bring back his dead brother Hisao ı the Ceremony. It should be pointed out that Jun is (was?) a star student at the school, one of Gribbs' favorites and a member of the inner circle that knew certain secrets about the way the Academy works, so his knowledge of the Ceremony is greater than ours. First appearing in issue #2 and something we saw him lead and initiate in issue #18 (where a sacrifice was also demanded), it's clear Jun has some idea of what he's doing, even if we're still unsure of what exactly the Ceremony does.

Of course, that Jun's sacrifice is Jade is instantly problematic, not just because she's a fan favorite and a main character that is alive in the future (issue #6) but because we've been down the resurrection road with her before in issue #34. While issue #33 showed us that a person's being could be transferred between bodies (hence the Junisao Conundrum), issue #34 definitively stated repeatedly that dead is dead and that you can't bring back that which is gone – and while we don't know the aftermath of #34's cliffhanger, we made plenty of assumptions that it involved bringing back an empty and disoriented shell since the "being" of a person would've been lost.

So with Jun's plan, we run into a interesting scenario in that we know it's doomed to fail and we're aware of the acute dramatic irony of attempting to use Jade as the sacrifice to bring back Hisao. That Jun wants to sacrifice a person is fairly interesting as last time their sacrifice was a goat; perhaps the bigger the sacrifice being offered, the greater the task you can accomplish. Not only that, but it's possible that Jun is aware of Jade's attempt to revive her mother given his previous involvement with the Academy; it's most likely coincidental, but perhaps he thinks that using her will offer them a unique entity through which to attempt to break this known taboo based on what she did previously.

GLORIES
by Joe Eisma

morningglory babies

MEYLIKHOV & EISMA

morningglory babies

MEYLIKHOV & EISMA

morningglory babies

MEYLIKHOV & EISMA